CW01467122

Shining Lights

Student's Book STARTER
Combo A
A1

David McKeegan   Helen Tiliouine

Oracy	Challenge	Life competencies	STEAM
Working with other students Showing your partner that you are listening	I want to find out more about the people in my class.	**Creative thinking:** preparing for creativity **Critical thinking:** evaluating ideas and arguments	**Science** Why are we all different?
▶️ **Asking questions** Asking for more information Asking for clarification		**Learning to learn:** developing skills and strategies for learning **Creative thinking:** generating ideas	
Talking about ideas with other people Making sure that people can hear you Presenting a poster Showing interest	I want to know more about the food I eat.	**Collaboration:** encouraging effective group interaction **Critical thinking:** evaluating ideas and arguments **Digital literacy:** using tools and creating digital content	**Science** How can I cook safely?
▶️ **Giving a presentation** Speaking slowly and clearly Using body language and making eye contact		**Emotional development:** empathy and relationship skills	
Asking for people's opinions about your ideas Taking turns	It's good to do new things!	**Critical thinking:** solving problems and making decisions **Creative thinking:** implementing ideas and solving problems **Critical thinking:** evaluating ideas and arguments **Critical thinking:** solving problems and making decisions	
Digital Classroom: Practice Extra			

WELCOME TO SHINING LIGHTS

Learn about the features in your new Student's Book.

ORACY
Learn the skills to become proficient when you communicate

VIDEO
Watch interesting videos that bring language to life

TALKING POINTS
Say what you think about the topics in the unit and listen to others' views

LEARNING AIMS
See what you will learn in this unit

CHALLENGE
Think about, research and resolve challenging issues

CHALLENGE: STAGE 1
Start thinking about the issue you will discuss throughout the unit, ending in a presentation of your findings and discussions

HOW IS UNIT 5 SO FAR?
Think about and reflect on what you've learned up until now

VIDEO
Watch interesting documentaries about a variety of topics

THINK OUTSIDE THE BOX
Read or listen to a text with unexpected ideas and think about it in an original and creative way

LIFE COMPETENCIES
Practise different skills with these tips and exercises

STRETCH!
Go a bit further – stretch yourself!

GRAMMAR VIDEO
Watch grammar videos to practise and improve your grammar

GRAMMAR BOX
Simple grammar explanations

DIGITAL ACTIVITIES
Go online to learn and practise more grammar

IMPROVE YOUR WRITING
Improve your writing following these simple steps

ORACY VIDEO
Watch real students practising their oracy skills and discussing how well they've done

ORACY
Combine and practise all of the oracy skills you've learned in this unit

EXAM TRAINING
Exam training and practice

EXAM TIP
Read through exam tips to improve your performance

SELF-ASSESSMENT
Reflect on how confident you are with what you've learned at the end of the unit

SUSTAINABILITY
Reflect on what you've learned about sustainability in this unit

CHALLENGE: STAGE 2
Start preparing the issue you will discuss throughout the unit, get into groups and start researching!

PRONUNCIATION
Improve your pronunciation by doing the digital exercises

CHALLENGE: STAGE 3
Develop your ideas further and prepare a first draft

ORACY
Improve and practise your skills to speak in public

STEAM INVESTIGATIONS
Learn more about STEAM (Science, Technology, Engineering, Arts and Maths) and investigate different issues

CHALLENGE: STAGE 4
Present your work to the class

GRAMMAR REFERENCE AND PRACTICE
See all of the grammar explained and practise it!

UNIT 1 WE'RE ALL DIFFERENT!

LEARNING AIMS

- **Skills**: talk and write about ourselves, ask people questions
- **Grammar**: learn and practise question words, possessive adjectives and the present simple of *be*
- **Vocabulary**: learn and practise words for people's favourite things and activities, numbers 0–20 and adjectives to describe things
- **Critical thinking**: find out about your classmates
- **Exam practice**: Reading Part 4, Writing Part 6, Listening Part 3

THE CHALLENGE

I want to find out more about the people in my class.
You will:

- **Stage 1 Think:** think about what information you want to find out.
- **Stage 2 Prepare:** write a questionnaire.
- **Stage 3 Develop:** ask your questions.
- **Stage 4 Present:** tell the class about your classmate.

FAVOURITE COLOUR: blue

FAVOURITE MUSIC: rock

FAVOURITE MONTH: June

FAVOURITE DAY: Saturday

FAVOURITE FOOD: chocolate

FAVOURITE DRINK: mango juice

FAVOURITE CITY: Paris

CHALLENGE ① ② ③ ④

Think

Work in pairs. Discuss the questions.

1 What is important to know about your classmates?

• their name	yes / no
• how old they are	yes / no
• their favourite music	yes / no
• things they do at the weekend	yes / no

2 Think of five or six more things to ask about.

1 Look at the photo. In pairs, discuss the questions.

1 Where are the people?
2 How old are they?

2 Watch the video. Where is Kasia from? Where is Trevor from?

 ▶ 01

Documentary

Grammar

| 7

VOCABULARY

FAVOURITE THINGS AND ACTIVITIES

1 🔊 **1.1 Write the words under the photos. Listen, check and repeat.**

band   bike   board game   camera   cinema   comic book
cycling   film   guitar   hiking   online gaming   party

2 ▶ 01 Watch the video again. What are Kasia and Trevor's favourite activities?

3 Read the text in Exercise 4 quickly. What is the girl's name? Where is she from?

☑ EXAM TRAINING READING PART 4

EXAM TIP

Each question has only one correct answer.

4 Read the text again. For each question, choose the correct answer.

‹ Inbox

Hi, my name's Ana! I'm 13 years old, and I live in Berlin. My favourite sport is cycling, and I go to school on my **(1)** _____ every day. At the weekends, I go to watch **(2)** _____ at the cinema with my friends. I also take great photos with my new **(3)** _____. This is a photo of me in my favourite place in my house!

1 A comic   B bike   C guitar
2 A books   B music   C films
3 A camera   B party   C band

5 Work in pairs. Ask and answer questions about your favourite things.

What's your favourite music / film / band / board game / comic book / online game?

NUMBERS 0–20

6 🔊 **1.2 Write the numbers next to the words. Then say the numbers in the correct order. Listen, check and repeat.**

three ____	seven ____	nine ____
one ____	ten ____	zero ____
four ____	two ____	six ____
five ____	eight ____	seventeen ____
twenty ____	eleven ____	nineteen ____
fourteen ____	twelve ____	fifteen ____
eighteen ____	sixteen ____	thirteen ____

7 Work in pairs. Say a number. Your partner writes it. Then your partner says a number and you write it.

twelve

12

READING

A CONVERSATION

1 **Look at the photos of Ben and Rosa. Do you think the sentences are true or false? Why?**

1 Ben plays the guitar.
2 Rosa's favourite colour is blue.

2 **Read the text in the box below. Answer the questions.**

1 Who is new at the school?
2 Are Rosa and Ben in the same class?
3 Where is the school?

> Rosa is a new student at Ben's school. Ben and Rosa are both in Class 8C. Their school is in Bristol, in England.

3 **Read Ben and Rosa's conversation quickly and check your answers to Exercise 1.**

4 🔊 **1.3 Read and listen to the conversation. Answer the questions.**

1 How old is Rosa? _____
2 Where is she from? _____
3 What is her favourite band?

_____

4 How old is Ben? _____
5 Where is he from? _____
6 What is his favourite colour?

_____

>>> **STRETCH!** **Work in pairs and follow the instructions.**

- Student A: Find photos of Rosa's city and information about it.
- Student B: Find photos of Ben's city and information about it.
- Tell each other what you find out.

Hi, I'm Ben! What's your name?

Rosa

What's your number?

Ben
Online

Hi!

Hi!

Where are you from?

Cartagena, in Colombia.

Cool!

I'm in Bristol because of my mum's new job at the university.

Great! Welcome to our school! And welcome to my city, Bristol! How old are you?

I'm 12. And you?

13.

Is that your guitar in the photo?

Yes, I'm in a small school band.

Really? Who's in the band with you?

A boy and a girl from Class 8C. His name is Leo and her name is Claire.

My favourite band is called Rancho Aparte.

Why do you like them?

Their music is fun and beautiful.

I'd like to hear some of it. But first, can I ask one thing?

What?

Your favourite colour is red, right?

Yes, it is! What's yours?

Yellow!

GRAMMAR

QUESTION WORDS

1 Complete the questions from Ben and Rosa's conversation.

1 _____'s your name?
2 _____ are you from?
3 _____ old are you?
4 _____'s in the band with you?
5 _____ do you like them?

2 Choose the correct answers to complete the rules in the grammar box.

> **Question words**
>
> We use question words at the [1] *end / beginning* of questions.
>
> We use [2] *what / how / who* with *old* to ask about people's age.
>
> ▶ Grammar reference and practice page 98

3 🖥 Go to the digital activities.

4 Write the question words.

1 _____ is your favourite actor?
2 _____ is she from?
3 _____ do you like that band?
4 _____ old is he?

POSSESSIVE ADJECTIVES

5 Complete the sentences from Ben and Rosa's conversation.

1 Welcome to _____ school!
2 _____ name is Leo and _____ name is Claire.
3 _____ favourite band is called Rancho Aparte.
4 _____ music is fun and beautiful.

6 Complete the rules with the words in the box.

> her   his   our   their   your

> **Possessive adjectives**
>
> The possessive adjectives for *I*, *you*, *she*, *he* and *it* are *my*, [1]_____ , [2]_____ , [3]_____ and *its*.
> The possessive adjectives for *we*, *you* and *they* are [4]_____ , *your* and [5]_____ .
>
> ▶ Grammar reference and practice page 98

7 🖥 Go to the digital activities.

8 Write the correct possessive adjective in each conversation.

1
Hi, _____ name's Evin.

Hello, Evin. I'm Gary.

2
Who's that?

_____ name's Paul. He's my friend.

3
Who's your favourite singer?

Taylor Swift. _____ songs are really good.

4
That's my pet mouse.

What's _____ name?

5
We like this class, and we like _____ teacher!

Great!

6
These are my cats!

Oh, what are _____ names?

9 Work in pairs. Ask and answer questions. Then write three sentences about your partner.

What's your name?   My name's Lucy.

Her name's Lucy.

CHALLENGE 1 2 3 4

Prepare

1 Work in groups of three or four. Remember to work together!
2 Look at the things you want to know about your classmates from Stage 1.
3 Decide how many questions you want in your questionnaire.
4 Write the questions for your questionnaire.

HOW IS UNIT 1 SO FAR?

☆☆☆ I understand   ☆☆ I'm getting there   ☆ I don't understand

Welcome to **my world!** *By Danny*

🛈 💡 **THINK OUTSIDE THE BOX!**

My name is Danny and I am 12 years old. I'm from York. York is a beautiful city in the north of England. It's not very big, but it's very old. My favourite films are *Enola Holmes 1* and *2*. My favourite actor is in them. His name is Louis Partridge. My favourite band is Imagine Dragons. Their music isn't boring; it's fun!

My friend's name is Rob. Our favourite activities are online gaming and cycling. Rob's new bike is expensive and very fast. My old bike is cheap and slow! Rob and I are in class 7B at school. Our school is small, and all our teachers are nice.

When Rob and I talk, we often use sign language. We also both have cochlear implants, so we can hear our teachers and our classmates. At home with my family, I use sign language because my parents are deaf, too. Rob and I also use sign language at parties with loud music. Sign language is very important for lots of people, and it's very important for me!

Can you spell your name in sign language?

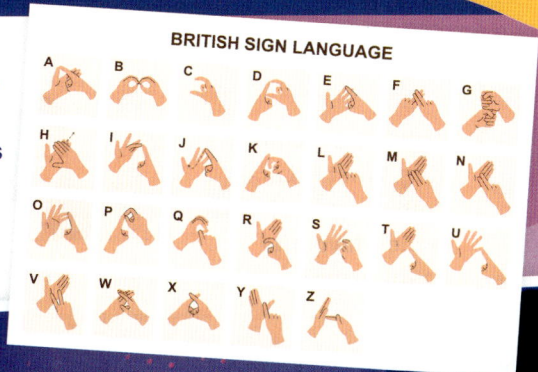
BRITISH SIGN LANGUAGE

READING

A BLOG POST

1 Look at the photo. What activity can you see?

2 🔊 1.4 Read and listen to the blog post. Answer the questions.

   1 Where is Danny from?

   2 What is his friend's name?

3 Read the blog post again. Complete the information.

Danny's favourite ...

   1 films _____

   2 actor _____

   3 band _____

   4 activities _____

4 Work in pairs. Use a dictionary to find the meaning of *cochlear implant*, *sign language* and *deaf*.

VOCABULARY

DESCRIBING THINGS

1 🔊 1.5 Write the correct adjective for each photo. Listen, check and repeat.

  beautiful   big   cheap   expensive   fast   fun   important   new   slow   small

a _____ party

a _____ animal

an _____ book

a _____ flower

a _____ tree

a _____ boy

a _____ camera

an _____ person

a _____ house

a _____ guitar

2 Which adjectives in Exercise 1 are opposites?

big / small

3 🛈 **Creative Thinking** Work in pairs. Think about things that are important or beautiful. Do you and your partner think the same?

GRAMMAR

PRESENT SIMPLE: BE

1 Watch the grammar vlog. What is Lara's brother's name? What is their favourite board game?

▶ 02

2 Look at the examples from the grammar vlog. Complete the rules in the grammar box.

- I **am** 12 years old.
- Lucas **is** 12.
- We **are** at the same school.
- **I'm not!**
- Lucas **is not** in class 7A.
- Parties **aren't** fun.
- **Is** it Scrabble?
- **Are** parties fun?

> am   are   before   is   not

Present simple: be

In **positive** sentences, we use I [1] _____ , you are, he/she/it [2] _____ , we/you/they [3] _____ .

In **negative** sentences, we add [4] _____ .

In **questions**, the verb be is [5] _____ the subject.

▶ Grammar reference and practice page 98

3 Go to the digital activities.

4 Choose the correct answers to complete the sentences.

1 *It / He* is an expensive camera.
2 *I / We* are in Class 7C.
3 *You / She* are my friend.
4 *They / It* are beautiful.
5 *He / I* am your friend.
6 *She / They* is from Egypt.

5 Write sentences with contractions (').

Example: You are in my class. _You're in my class_ .

1 We are in Mexico. _____
2 I am not ten. _____
3 They are our friends. _____
4 He is our teacher. _____
5 It is not cheap. _____
6 You are not old. _____

6 Put the words in the correct order.

1 from / They / Italy / aren't / .
2 he / your / Is / friend / ?
3 not / I / in England / am / .
4 your / fast / bike / Is / ?
5 my / Are / in / you / class / ?
6 Spain / My sister / in / is / .

7 PRONUNCIATION Go to the digital pronunciation activity.

8 Complete the conversations.

1 **A:** Are you 13?
   B: No, I'm _____ , I'm 12.
2 **A:** Is your guitar expensive?
   B: Yes, it _____ .
3 **A:** _____ Scrabble your favourite board game?
   B: No, it _____ .
4 **A:** _____ you my friend?
   B: Yes, I _____ !

9 Work in pairs. Ask and answer questions with *be*.

Are you 14?

Yes, I am. / No, I'm not, I'm ...

10 Critical Thinking Lara and Lucas are twins. Think about being a twin. Work in pairs. How many good and bad things can you think of?

DIGITAL CLASSROOM

PRACTICE EXTRA UNIT 1

CHALLENGE 1 2 3 4

Develop

1 Choose someone in a different group to interview.
2 Ask your classmate the questions in your questionnaire.
3 Write down the answers.

WRITING

AN EMAIL

1 Imagine a new online friend. Fill in the information about your new friend.

- Name: _____
- Age: _____
- City/Country: _____, _____
- Favourite activity, music, film:

  _____, _____,

  _____

2 Read the email from your new friend. Complete the email with information from Exercise 1.

> ‹ Inbox   ∧ ∨
>
> Hi your name,
>
> My name's _____ and I'm
> _____ years old. I'm from
> _____, in _____.
> _____ is a beautiful _____.
> My school's small and my lessons are fun. My
> favourite activity is _____. My favourite
> music is _____, and my favourite film is
> _____.
>
> What are your favourite things?
>
> Write soon,
>
> _____

3 Match the items in the email plan (1–6) to the phrases from the email (a–f).

Email plan:

1 Start the email.
2 Give information about my town/city.
3 Give information about my school.
4 Give information about my favourite things.
5 Ask a question.
6 End the email.

a What are your favourite things?
b ... is a beautiful ... .
c Write soon, ...
d My school's small and my lessons are fun.
e Hi ... ,
f My favourite activity is ... . My favourite music is ... , and my favourite film is ... .

4 Read the exam task in Exercise 6. How many things do you need to write about in your email to Sam?

5 Look at the email in Exercise 2. <u>Underline</u> the sentences which can help you to write your email.

☑ EXAM TRAINING WRITING PART 6

EXAM TIP

In your answer, always write about the three things in the exam task.

6 You have a new online friend called Sam. Write an email to Sam.

Tell Sam about:
- your town or city
- your school
- your favourite music.

Write **20 words** or more.

7 Read your email again and check your work. Use these questions to help you.

1 Is there information about:
   - your town or city?
   - your school?
   - your favourite music?
2 Is there a good start and end to the email?
3 Is the spelling and grammar correct?

8 Now work in pairs. Read each other's emails and give feedback. Use the questions in Exercise 7 to help you. Make a note of your partner's feedback and write a second draft of your email.

>> **STRETCH!** Write an answer to the email in Exercise 2.

CHALLENGE —①—②—③—④

Present

1 Tell the class about your classmate.
   - Talk for around one minute.
   - Answer other students' questions.
2 Listen carefully to other students. Ask a question if you want.

LISTENING

A CONVERSATION

1 Work in pairs. Look at the photo. Who is in the photo?

2 🔊 1.6 You will hear Rosa talking to her classmate, Anatol. Listen to the first part of their conversation. How many names of countries do you hear? Which countries are they?

3 Look at the exam question below. Listen again and read the script. Choose the correct answer. Why are the other answers wrong?

> 1 Where is Anatol from?
> **A** Poland   **B** England   **C** Colombia

Anatol: Hello!

Rosa: Hi! What's your name? I'm Rosa, from Colombia. It's my first day at your school.

Anatol: Really? I'm Anatol, from Poland.

Rosa: Oh, so like me, you aren't from England.

☑ EXAM TRAINING   LISTENING PART 3

EXAM TIP

In Listening Part 3, there are always two people having a conversation. They talk about question 1 first, then question 2, etc. You always hear everything twice in the Listening exam.

4 🔊 1.7 Now listen to the rest of the conversation. For each question, choose the correct answer.

> 2 What are Rosa's favourite books about?
> **A** sport   **B** music   **C** animals
> 3 Anatol's bike is
> **A** new.   **B** beautiful.   **C** expensive.

5 Listen again and check your answers.

ORACY

Showing your partner that you are listening

When your partner says something, use words like *Oh / Really? / Great!* to show that you are interested. Look at them and smile.

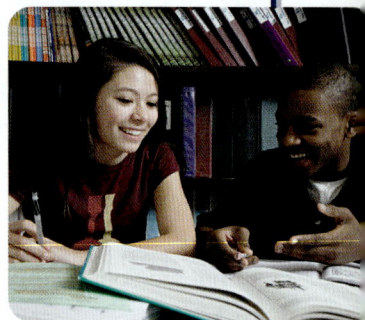

6 Look at the script in Exercise 3 again. Underline the words that Rosa and Anatol use to show that they are interested. Check your answers in pairs.

>>> STRETCH! Work in groups of three or four. Choose a book to read or a film to watch. Next week, tell each other what you think about the book or the film. Remember to show that you are interested!

SELF-ASSESSMENT: UNIT 1

How confident do you feel about:

- talking about your favourite things and activities?
- using question words?
- using the verb *be*?
- talking about yourself and other people?
- asking people questions about themselves?
- planning ideas before you write?
- showing you are interested when you listen?

What was your favourite part of Unit 1? Tell your partner.

_____

_____

UNIT 2 MY PEOPLE

LEARNING AIMS

Skills: describe people

Grammar: learn and practise *this / that / these / those*, possessive *'s* and *have(n't) got*

Vocabulary: learn and practise words for family members and adjectives to describe people

Oracy: ask questions

Exam practice: Reading Part 5, Listening Part 1

ORACY

Asking questions

- asking for more information
- asking for clarification

1 Look at the photo. In pairs, discuss the questions.

1 Who are the people?

2 Why are they happy?

2 Watch the video. Are the sentences true or false?

1 All animals like to live in groups.

2 People like to be in groups, but sometimes they also like to be alone.

3 In general, people have fun when they are together.

3 Work in pairs. Read the statements below.
Student A: Say which statements are true for you.
Student B: Ask one question about each statement. Then change roles.

- My family is really interesting.
- It's sometimes fun to be alone.

4 Think about your discussion. Why is it important to ask questions in a conversation?

Documentary

Grammar

Oracy

VOCABULARY

FAMILY MEMBERS

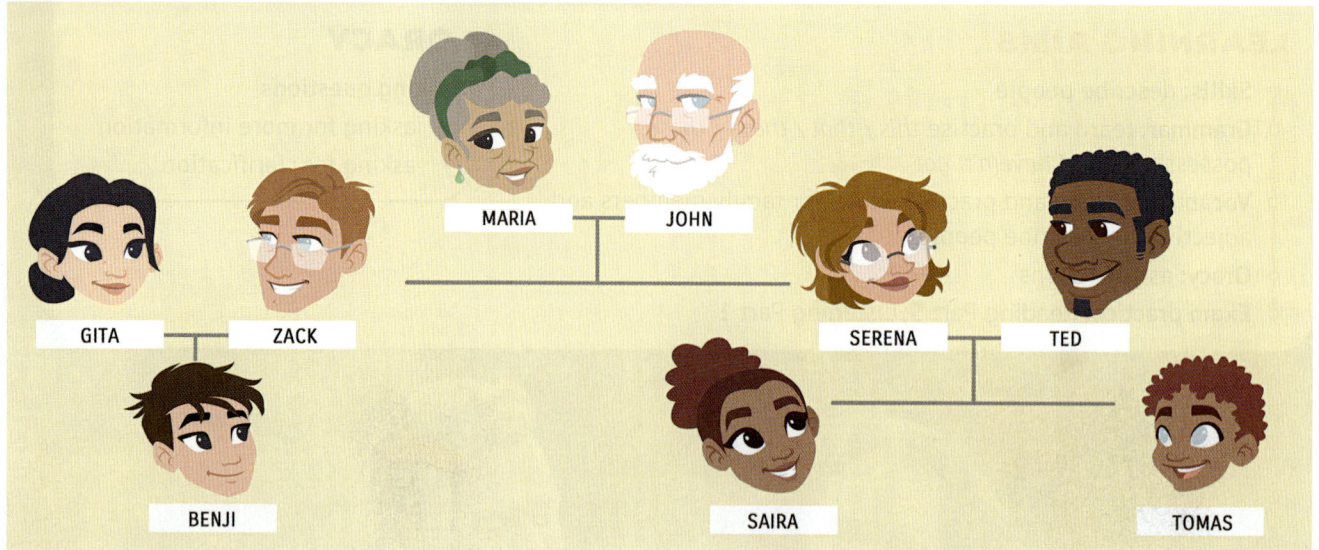

MARIA — JOHN

GITA — ZACK

SERENA — TED

BENJI

SAIRA

TOMAS

1 Look at Saira's family tree. Complete her blog post with the words.

aunt   ~~brother~~   cousin   dad   daughter
grandma   grandpa   mum   sister   son   uncle

Hi, I'm Saira. My little ¹ _____brother_____ is called Tomas. He's only six years old. My ² _____ is called Ted and my ³ _____ is called Serena. I've got one ⁴ _____ – his name is Zack. My mother is Zack's ⁵ _____ . Zack is married to my ⁶ _____ , Gita. Their ⁷ _____ is called Benji. He's an only child. He's my ⁸ _____ .
He's eleven years old, and he's great fun! My ⁹ _____ is called Maria, and my ¹⁰ _____ is called John. My mother is their ¹¹ _____ .
We're a happy family!

2 🔊 2.1 Listen and check your answers.

3 Choose the correct answers to complete the sentences.

1   Your uncle's son is your *aunt / brother / cousin*.
2   Your father's mother is your *grandma / aunt / sister*.
3   Your mother's sister is your *cousin / grandma / aunt*.
4   Your cousin's father is your *father / uncle / grandpa*.
5   Your mother's daughter is your *sister / brother / grandma*.
6   Your father's father is your *uncle / grandpa / cousin*.

4 Read the text. Are the sentences true or false?

Is your family very big? Jenna Ortega's is! She's an American actor, famous for being in the TV show *Wednesday*. She has two brothers (Isaac and Markus) and three sisters (Mariah, Mia and Aaliyah). Their parents are called Natalie and Edward. One of Jenna's sisters, Mariah, has her own children now.

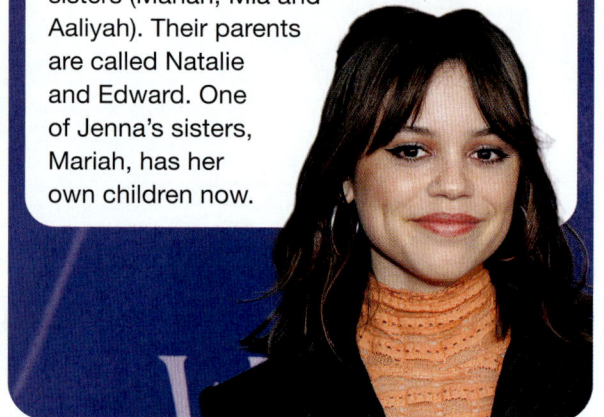

1   Jenna is Natalie and Edward's daughter.
2   Edward is Natalie's father.
3   Natalie is a grandmother.
4   Jenna is an aunt.
5   Isaac is Mariah's sister.
6   Markus is an uncle.

5 🗣 PRONUNCIATION Go to the digital pronunciation activity.

6 🔵 Learning to Learn Work in pairs. Use a dictionary to find these family words in English. Write sentences about Saira's family using these words.

1   What is the English word for the daughter of your brother or sister? What is the word for their son?
2   What is a married man called? What is a married woman called?

READING

BLOG POSTS

1 Look at the photos of two families. Who are the people? Where are they?

2 Read the blog posts quickly. Match the posts to the photos.

BLOGS ⌄   NEWSLETTERS ⌄   VIDEOS ⌄

PAULA

This is a photo of me and my family. That's me in the middle, and the girl behind me is my sister. We are from a city called Zaragoza, in Spain. That's my dad with the camera. It's my parents' camera. My dad is an English teacher in my school. My mum is a taxi driver. My grandpa is in the photo, too. He's a doctor, but he isn't from Spain. My grandpa is from Portugal.

LUCAS

This is a photo of me, my cousin and some of our family. We're from Brazil. That's me next to the girl with the cat. She's my cousin, Loli. Those are her parents behind her. Loli plays the piano. These are my parents next to me. Their names are Paulo and Teresa. They are both doctors. My aunt is the tall person. Oh, and that's my grandpa behind me. It's my grandpa's cat!

3 🔊 **2.2** Read and listen to the blog posts. Choose the correct answers.

1 My dad's wife is a taxi driver. *Paula / Lucas*
2 My grandpa is from a different country. *Paula / Lucas*
3 My cousin plays music. *Paula / Lucas*
4 My dad is a teacher. *Paula / Lucas*
5 My mother and father are doctors. *Paula / Lucas*

ORACY

Taking turns

Wait for the other person to finish speaking before you speak.

4 Work in pairs and follow the instructions. Don't forget to wait for your partner to finish speaking before you speak.

- Student A: Show your partner a photo or a drawing of your family.
- Student B: Ask your partner questions about the photo.
- Then change roles.

Is this your grandpa?   Yes, it is.

How old is he?   He's 65.

>> STRETCH! Write a blog post about the photo or drawing of your family in Exercise 4. Who are they? How old are they? What do they do?

GRAMMAR

THIS, THAT, THESE, THOSE

1 Complete the sentences from the blog posts.

1 _____ is a photo of me and my family.
2 _____'s me next to the girl with the cat.
3 _____ are my parents next to me.
4 _____ are her parents behind her.

2 Choose the correct answers to complete the rules in the grammar box.

> **this, that, these, those**
>
> We use **this** and **that** for [1] plural / singular nouns.
> We use **these** and **those** for [2] plural / singular nouns.
> We use **this** and **these** for things that are [3] near to / far from us.
> We use **that** and **those** for things that are [4] near to / far from us.
>
> ▶ Grammar reference and practice page 99

3 🖥 Go to the digital activities.

4 Complete the sentences with *this, that, these* or *those*.

_____This_____ is my camera.

Is _____ your brother's guitar?

_____ is my bus.

_____ are my aunts' books.

_____'s my bicycle!

Are _____ your friends?

5 Work in pairs. Point to things in your classroom and ask questions.

> Is this your pen?
>
> No, it isn't.
>
> Who is that?
>
> That's our teacher.
>
> What is this?

POSSESSIVE 'S

6 Complete the sentences from Paula's and Lucas's blog posts.

1 It's my _____ cat!
2 It's my _____ camera.

7 Choose the correct answers to complete the rules in the grammar box.

> **Possessive 's**
>
> We use [1] verb / noun + 's to talk about possession.
> *Is that your brother's guitar?* = the guitar of my [2] brother / brothers
> When there is more than one person, we use only an apostrophe (').
> *These are my aunts' books.* = the books of my [3] aunt / aunts.
>
> ▶ Grammar reference and practice page 99

8 🖥 Go to the digital activities.

9 Rewrite the sentences with the apostrophe (') in the correct place.

1 What is your best friends name?
   _____
2 What colour is your mothers hair?
   _____
3 Karas uncle is a teacher.
   _____
4 Those boys teacher is Mr Benson.
   _____
5 What is your dads favourite sport?
   _____
6 Are these Tinas books?
   _____

ORACY

Asking for clarification

When you don't understand what someone says, you can say: *Sorry, I don't understand* or *Can you repeat that, please?*

10 Work in pairs and follow the instructions.

- Student A: Talk about your best friend. Tell your partner their name, hair colour, favourite sport and the number of people in their family.
- Student B: Ask for clarification if you need to.
- Then change roles.

HOW IS UNIT 2 SO FAR?

☆☆☆ I understand   ☆☆ I'm getting there   ☆ I don't understand

READING

AN ARTICLE

1 Work in pairs. Make a list of TV shows and films about families. How many can you think of?

2 Look at the example answer (0) at the beginning of the article. What grammar point does it test?

   A article   **B** verb   **C** pronoun

THE ADDAMS FAMILY

You know Wednesday Addams, the unusual girl from **(0)** _____*the*_____ TV show. But do you know the original TV show? **(1)** _____ is really old!

All of the Addams family are unusual. Wednesday's father's name is Gomez. He is rich. His hair is curly, and he **(2)** _____ got a moustache. He loves Wednesday's mother **(3)** _____ much.

Wednesday's mother is called Morticia. She has got **long**, **dark** hair. She is very clever.

Wednesday has got a little brother called Pugsley. He's got **short** hair. He loves to eat.

Uncle Fester is Wednesday's uncle. He hasn't got any hair at all! He likes to wear a very big coat all the time.

Grandma Addams is very old. She's got **long**, grey hair. She's Gomez's mother.

And there is Lurch. He isn't a member of the Addams family. He just works in their house, cooking and cleaning. He is very **tall**.

☑ EXAM TRAINING ‹ READING PART 5

EXAM TIP

Always read all the sentences before you write the answer.

3 Read the first two paragraphs of the article. For each question, write the correct answer. Write ONE word for each gap.

4 🔊 2.3 Read and listen to the whole article. Label the picture with the correct names.

5 Read the article again. Are the sentences true or false?

  1 Gomez has got a moustache.
  2 Pugsley's hair is long.
  3 Uncle Fester has got short hair.
  4 Lurch is small.

VOCABULARY

DESCRIBING PEOPLE

1 🔊 2.4 Choose the correct adjective for the photos. Listen, check and repeat.

1	2	3	4	5
long / short hair	long / short hair	blonde / dark hair	blonde / dark hair	curly / straight hair

6	7	8	9	10
curly / straight hair	old / young man	old / young girl	tall / short man	tall / short woman

2 🛡 Creative Thinking Work in pairs. Create your own TV family. Write a description of each person. What do they look like? What do they like to do?

GRAMMAR
HAVE(N'T) GOT

1 Watch the grammar vlog. What does Marco want?

▶ 02

2 Complete the sentences from the grammar vlog.

1 I _____ a big family.
2 I _____ a sister.
3 My friend Dan _____ two sisters.
4 He _____ any brothers.
5 _____ you _____ a scooter?

3 Choose the correct answers to complete the rules in the grammar box.

> ### have(n't) got
>
> We use *have got* to talk about possession.
> It means the same as *have*.
> We use *has/have got* + ¹ *noun / verb*.
> To ask questions, we use *Have/Has* + ² *noun / pronoun + got ... ?*
>
> ▶ Grammar reference and practice page 99

4 🖥 Go to the digital activities.

5 Choose the correct answers to complete the sentences.

1 We *haven't / hasn't* got many friends.
2 My sister *has / have* got blonde hair.
3 *Have / Has* you got a brother?
4 My parents *haven't / hasn't* got a car.
5 *Have / Has* Sally got long hair?

6 Look at the photo. Use the notes to write questions and answers.

1 Oscar / long hair?

> *Has Oscar got long hair?*

> *No, he hasn't.*

2 Luna / short hair?

3 Oscar / mobile phone?

4 Luna / curly hair?

5 Oscar and Luna / red hair?

6 Oscar and Luna / bicycles?

7 Work in pairs. Ask and answer questions about what people in your family have got. Use some of the ideas below and your own ideas.

long hair   car
computer   TV
garden   cat
moustache

> Has your mother got a car?

> Yes, she has.

▶▶▶ **STRETCH!** In pairs, play a game.

- Student A: Think of a person in your class or your family.
- Student B: Ask questions to find out who it is.
- Then change roles.

> Has he got blond hair?

> Is he tall?

> Is it Carlos?

DIGITAL CLASSROOM
PRACTICE EXTRA UNIT 2

WRITING

AN EMAIL

1 **Read the email. Who is Tania?**

   a Sally's online friend

   b a member of Sally's family

> ‹ **Inbox**   ∧ ∨
>
> Hi Tania,
>
> I want to tell you about my friends and family.
>
> My father is a teacher in my school, and my mother is an actor. She is very beautiful. I've got two little brothers. Their names are Noah and Saul. I've also got a dog called Molly.
>
> My best friend is called Jacinda. She's very tall, and she's got short, blonde hair.
>
> Best wishes,
>
> Sally

2 **Answer the questions.**

   1 What is Sally's father's job?
     He's a teacher.

   2 What is Sally's mother's job?

   3 Has Sally got any sisters?

   4 How many brothers has Sally got?

   5 Is Jacinda short?

   6 Has Jacinda got blonde hair?

3 **Complete the table with the phrases in the box.**

> Best wishes   Bye for now   ~~Dear Sasha~~
> Hello   Hi   Take care

Starting an email	Ending an email
Dear Sasha	

4 **Write a reply to Sally's email. Answer the questions. Don't forget to start and end your email correctly.**

   • What job has your father/mother got?

   • Have you got brothers and sisters?

   • Who is your best friend? What do they look like?

5 **Read your email again and check your work. Use these questions to help you.**

   1 Is there a good start and end to the email?

   2 Are there answers for all the questions?

   3 Are sentences with *have got/has got* correct?

   4 Is the spelling and grammar correct?

6 **Now work in pairs. Read each other's emails and give feedback. Use the questions in Exercise 5 to help you. Make a note of your partner's feedback and write a second draft of your email.**

LISTENING

SHORT DIALOGUES

1 **Work in pairs. Describe the men in the pictures.**

2 🔊 **2.5 Listen to the conversation. Which man is the boy's uncle? Choose the correct picture (A–C).**

3 **Read the questions and look at the pictures in Exercise 4. Say what you see in each picture.**

> ☑ **EXAM TRAINING** ‹ **LISTENING PART 1**
>
> **EXAM TIP**
>
> Before you listen, read the questions. Look at each picture. What can you see?

4 🔊 **2.6 For each question, choose the correct answer.**

   1 Which is Lucia's family?

   2 What has Dan's mother got in her bag?

5 **Compare your answers with a partner. Then listen again and check your answers.**

ORACY

ASKING QUESTIONS
- asking for more information
- asking for clarification

1 Do you know your family tree? How big is it?

2 Match the questions (1–6) to the answers (a–f).

1 Are these the photos of your family?
2 How many brothers have you got?
3 Can you repeat that?
4 What colour hair has your father got?
5 Is that right?
6 How old is she?

a I've got two.
b Yes, they are.
c Yes, it is.
d Sorry, yes.
e She's 75.
f Brown.

3 Work in pairs. Which questions in Exercise 2 ask for more information? Which questions ask for clarification?

4 Watch the video. Which questions from Exercise 2 does Daniella ask? Are they to ask for more information or for clarification? ▶ 03

5 ▶ 04 Watch the rest of the video. What does Daniella say when she doesn't understand something?

6 Work in pairs. Watch the second part of the video again and make a list of all the questions Daniella asks. Put them in the correct column.

Asking for more information	Asking for clarification

7 Work in pairs. Ask and answer questions about each other's family. Make your partner's family tree.

What's your mum's name? — Tania.

What's your dad's name? — Rico.

How many brothers have you got?

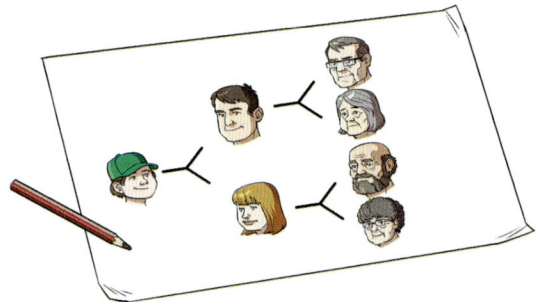

SELF-ASSESSMENT: UNIT 2

How confident do you feel about:
- talking about members of your family?
- writing about your family and friends?
- using *this, that, these* and *those*?
- describing how people look?
- asking and answering about what you and others *have(n't) got*?
- writing a short email?
- working on a task with your partner?
- using questions to ask for information and clarification?

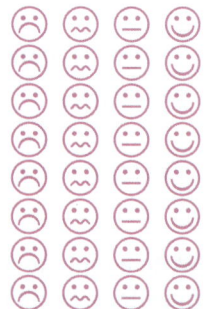

What was your favourite part of Unit 2? Tell your partner.

_____
_____

UNIT 3 LET'S EAT!

LEARNING AIMS

- **Skills**: talk about food, drink and containers, and quantities
- **Grammar**: learn about countable and uncountable nouns and practise *there is (not) / there are (not)*, *Is there / Are there* questions, *some / any / much / many / a lot of*
- **Vocabulary**: learn and practise words for food, drink and containers, and numbers 20–100
- **Critical thinking**: find information about food
- **Exam practice**: Reading Part 2, Listening Part 3, Speaking Part 1

THE CHALLENGE

I want to know more about the food I eat.
You will:

- **Stage 1 Think:** choose the food for your poster.
- **Stage 2 Prepare:** find out about this food.
- **Stage 3 Develop:** make a poster about the food.
- **Stage 4 Present:** show the poster to the class and talk about it.

1 **Look at the photo. In pairs, discuss the questions.**

1 Where are the people?
2 Do you think the food is nice? Why? / Why not?

2 **Watch the video. How many different types of bread are in the video? Is your favourite type of bread in the video?**

▶ 01

CHALLENGE — 1 - 2 - 3 - 4

Think

Work in small groups. Discuss the questions.

1 What's your favourite food?
2 What food is good and important for people?
3 Choose one kind of food to find out about.

Documentary

Grammar

VOCABULARY

FOOD, DRINK AND CONTAINERS

1 🔊 **3.1 Label the picture with the words. Listen, check and repeat.**

bottle   bowl   fruit   glass   juice   milkshake   noodles
plate   salad   sandwich   soup   vegetables

2 Work in pairs. Complete the word clouds with the words from Exercise 1.

FOOD

DRINK

CONTAINER
bottle

3 Complete the rules with *countable*, *uncountable*, *singular* (x 2) or *plural*.

Some nouns, like *bowl* and *egg*, are
¹ _____, for example *one*, *two*, *three*
eggs. Countable nouns can be ² _____ or
³ _____.

Some nouns, for example *chocolate* and *sugar*,
are ⁴ _____. These nouns can only be
⁵ _____.

ORACY

Talking about ideas with other people

We listen to each other. We ask questions.

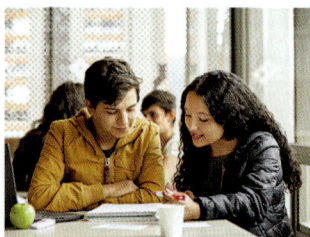

4 📷 **PRONUNCIATION** Go to the digital pronunciation activity.

5 Work in pairs. Ask and answer the questions.

What is your favourite food?

What are your favourite drinks?

⟫ **STRETCH!** Work in pairs. Add more words to the FOOD, DRINK and CONTAINER word clouds in Exercise 2. Use an online dictionary if you need to.

CHALLENGE —1—2—3—4

Prepare

1 Work in the same groups as for Stage 1.
2 Where is there information about the food you want to find out about? Is it in a book? Is it online?
3 Find information about this food. Where is the food from? Is it from a tree? Is it cheap or expensive? Do you need to cook it? Remember to listen to each other and to ask questions!

SHORT TEXTS

1 Work in pairs. Complete the table with the words in the box. Use a dictionary to help you.

gluten-free
vegan   vegetarian

		meat	cheese, milk, yoghurt, etc.	wheat flour: bread, cakes, pasta
	1 I'm a _____ .	✗	✓	✓
	2 I'm a _____ .	✗	✗	✓
	3 I eat _____ food.	✓	✓	✗

2 🔊 3.2 Read and listen to the teenagers' blog posts. Who is vegan? Who eats gluten-free food?

BLOGS BY TEENAGE CHEFS

Keri

There is no meat or fish in the food I cook, and no milk or cheese! I am vegan. I use a lot of different vegetables and make really nice meals for my parents, my brothers and my sister. Potatoes are our favourite food. I've got my grandmother's cookbook. There are beautiful photos in it of salads and fruit! I've also got my grandmother's old, cheap camera!

Yann

My favourite activity is cooking! I make big meals for my friends and family. My parents like all kinds of food, but my big sister's favourite food is vegetable noodles, and my two little sisters love ice cream. All my food is gluten-free. I've got a very good camera – it isn't cheap! I want to write a cookbook with lots of great photos of my food in it!

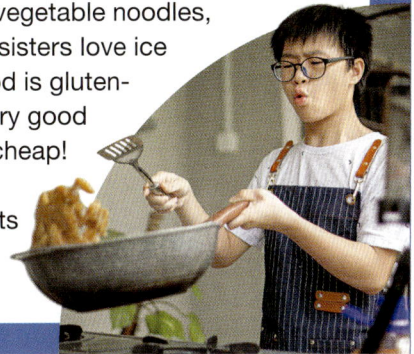

EXAM TIP

Read each question so you know which information to look for. Underline the important words in each question. Then look at what Keri and Yann say to find the information you need.

3 Look at question 1 in Exercise 5. What are the important words in the question?

4 Read the blog posts again and answer the questions.

1 Read Keri's blog. Is there any information about a book?
2 Now read Yann's blog. Is there any information about a book?
3 Who has got a nice book? Why is it nice?

✅ EXAM TRAINING READING PART 2

5 Now look at questions 2–4. For each question, choose the correct answer.

		Keri	Yann
1	Who has got a nice book?	A	B
2	Who has got an expensive camera?	A	B
3	Who has got three sisters?	A	B
4	Who has got a favourite vegetable?	A	B

6 🏛 Collaboration Work in groups of three or four. Make a list of vegan food OR gluten-free food. Use a dictionary or look online. Tell another group what you find out.

GRAMMAR

THERE IS / ARE, THERE ISN'T / AREN'T

1 Watch the grammar vlog. What does Lara want to make? Has she got everything she needs?

 ▶ 02

2 Look at the examples from the grammar vlog. Complete the rules with the words in the box.

- **There is a** bowl.
- **There is some** flour.
- **There are some** eggs: one, two, three eggs!
- **There isn't a** candle.
- **There isn't any** chocolate.
- **There aren't any** strawberries.

> a/an   any x2   some x2

there is / are, there isn't / aren't

- **there is** + ¹ _____ + singular countable noun (like *bowl, egg*)
- **there is** + ² _____ + uncountable noun (like *flour, sugar*)
- **there are** + ³ _____ + plural countable noun (like *bowls, eggs*)
- **there isn't** + a/an + singular countable noun
- **there isn't** + ⁴ _____ + uncountable noun
- **there aren't** + ⁵ _____ + plural countable noun

▶ Grammar reference and practice page 100

3 🖥 Go to the digital activities.

4 Complete the sentences with *is / are / isn't / aren't*.

1 There _____ any sandwiches.
2 There _____ some soup.
3 There _____ any salad.
4 There _____ some vegetables.

5 Choose the correct answers.

1 There are *any / some* potatoes.
2 There isn't *any / a* bread.
3 There's *some / a* water.
4 There isn't *any / a* bowl.
5 There aren't *some / any* oranges.
6 There is *an / one* plate.

6 Work in pairs. Say sentences. Then write the sentences.

✓ *There's some water.*   ✗ _____

✗ _____   ✓ _____

✓ _____   ✗ _____

ORACY

Making sure that people can hear you

Project your voice to speak clearly.

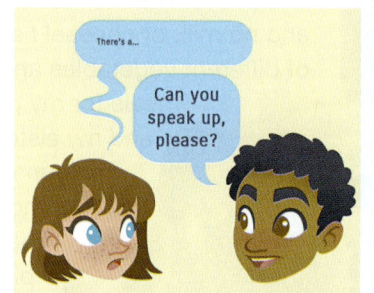

7 Work in pairs. Follow the instructions.

- Student A: Look at the picture on page 109 for 30 seconds. Cover the picture and tell Student B what you remember.
- Student B: Look at the picture on page 108 for 30 seconds. Cover the picture and tell Student A what you remember.
- Remember to speak clearly.

> There's a ...   There are four ...

8 Complete the sentences with your own ideas. Share your ideas with a classmate.

In my kitchen, there's a _____, and there's some _____. There isn't a _____, there isn't any _____, and there aren't any _____.

HOW IS UNIT 3 SO FAR?

☆☆☆ I understand   ☆☆ I'm getting there   ☆ I don't understand

VOCABULARY

NUMBERS 20–100

1 🔊 **3.3 Look and match the words (1–9) to the photos (a–i). Listen, check and repeat.**

1	twenty strawberries	6	seventy pineapples
2	thirty bananas	7	eighty carrots
3	forty lemons	8	ninety coconuts
4	fifty tomatoes	9	a hundred peas
5	sixty beans		

2 🔊 **3.4 Listen and write the numbers.**

3 Which words in Exercise 1 are fruit? Which are vegetables?

4 Work in pairs. Student A: Write a number. Student B: Say the number. Then change roles.

>>> **STRETCH!** Work in pairs. How do you say 1,000 in English? And 10,000? 100,000? 1,000,000? Use a dictionary or look online to find out.

a	20	b	70	c	40
d	90	e	30	f	60
g	80	h	50	i	100

LISTENING

AN INTERVIEW

1 Look at the photos. What food can you see?

2 Read the introduction to the interview. Are the sentences true or false?

1 The farm is in a city.
2 Tomas works at the farm.

A special farm

There aren't many farms in cities. But in Paris, the capital city of France, there's a farm on a roof! Tomas, 13, is visiting the farm with his English class. He wants to make a podcast about the farm in English.

3 🔊 **3.5 Listen to Tomas talking to an English woman who works on the farm. Is there any fruit on the farm? Are there any vegetables?**

✓ EXAM TRAINING — LISTENING PART 3

EXAM TIP

For each question in Listening Part 3, you hear all the answers (A, B, C), but only one is the correct answer.

4 Listen to the interview again. For each question, choose the correct answer.

1 How many strawberries are there in the woman's box?
   A 20   **B** 50   **C** 70

2 Tomas thinks the tomatoes are
   A small.   **B** beautiful.   **C** expensive.

5 Compare your answers with a partner. Then listen again and check.

6 🎓 **Critical Thinking** Work in small groups. Choose a country. Find out the different types of food that people eat there. Answer the questions.

- What is a really important food for people in that country?
- Choose three important things about the food.
- Write three sentences about the food.

GRAMMAR

IS THERE / ARE THERE QUESTIONS, *MUCH, MANY, A LOT (OF)*

1 Complete the questions and answers from Tomas's interview.

1 How _____ fruit is there?
2 There _____ much.
3 How _____ strawberries are there?
4 Are there _____ tomatoes?
5 There are _____ tomatoes.

2 Complete the rules in the grammar box.

> **Is there / Are there** questions, *much / many / a lot (of)*
>
> Questions about **countable** nouns:
> ¹ _____ there any apples?
> Is there ² _____ table in your kitchen?
> How ³ _____ bananas are there?
> Questions about **uncountable** nouns:
> ⁴ _____ there any water?
> How ⁵ _____ bread is there?
> We can use *a* ⁶ _____ *of* with countable **and** uncountable nouns.
>
> ▶ Grammar reference and practice page 100

3 🖥 Go to the digital activities.

4 Complete the sentences with *much* or *many*.

1 There isn't _____ soup.
2 How _____ bottles are there?
3 Are there _____ noodles?
4 There aren't _____ plates.
5 How _____ bread is there?

5 Put the words in the correct order.

1 pasta / How / there / much / is / ?
2 there / vegetables / any / Are / ?
3 aren't / strawberries / many / There / .
4 lot / salad / There / of / a / is .
5 many / are / oranges / there / How / ?
6 much / There / cheese / isn't /.
7 a / Is / small box / there / on the table / ?

6 Work in pairs. Ask and answer questions with *How much? / How many?*

How many apples are there?

There are two. / There aren't many.

1 2 3

SPEAKING

ANSWERING QUESTIONS ABOUT YOURSELF

EXAM TIP

In Speaking Part 1, you answer some questions about yourself. Use complete sentences to answer the questions.

Where are you from? ✓ I'm from São Paulo. ✗ from here

1 🔊 3.6 Listen to two students doing part of the Speaking exam. Do they use complete sentences to answer the questions?

2 Work in pairs. Write six or seven questions using the words below.

where **how** what **how many** is there / are there

name **old** from favourite actor / food / etc. **students in your class** **milk in fridge**

Where are you from?

☑ EXAM TRAINING SPEAKING PART 1

3 Work in pairs. Take turns to ask and answer your questions from Exercise 2.

CHALLENGE 1 2 3 4

Develop

1 Make your poster in your group.
2 Draw a picture of the food.
3 Write some sentences about the food.

WRITING

A MESSAGE

1 Read David's message about a party. Who is the party for?

David
Online

Hi Mum!

We need some 🥚🥚 eggs for a cake for Grandma's party. And we haven't got any 🌾 flour.

There's some sugar, but there isn't any 🧈 butter. And we need a lot of 🕯️ candles! And some balloons!

I also want to make a fruit salad, but there isn't much fruit. There aren't many bananas and there aren't any strawberries.

Can you get what we need at the shops, please?

Thanks,

David

2 Read the message again and complete David's mother's shopping list.

- *eggs*
- *flour*
-
-
-
-
-

3 Work in pairs. Imagine you want to have a party for a friend's birthday. Write a list of things that you need for the party.

-
-
-
-
-
-
-
-
-
-

4 What things on your list in Exercise 3 have you got at home? Cross them out.

~~sugar~~

5 Look at David's message again. Answer the questions.

1 How does David start and end his message?
2 Underline the parts of the message that tell David's mother what they need for the party.

6 Write a message to someone in your family. Look at your list in Exercise 3 and ask the person to buy the things you need. Write 35–70 words.

7 Read your message again and check your work. Use these questions to help you.

1 Is there information about what you need for the party?
2 Is there a good start and end to the message?
3 Is the spelling and grammar correct?

8 Now work in pairs. Read each other's messages and give feedback. Use the questions in Exercise 7 to help you. Make a note of your partner's feedback and write a second draft of your message.

>>> STRETCH! Work in pairs. Plan a party for your class. What do you need for the party?

ORACY

Presenting a poster

When you present a poster to the class, stand next to the poster so the other students can see it. Don't stand in front of the poster!

CHALLENGE — 1 2 3 4

Present

1 Choose one person in your group to present your poster to the class.
2 To practise, the person presents the poster to your group.
   - Listen carefully.
   - Think: What is good about the presentation? What is not so good? Where is the person standing?
   - Give the person feedback.
3 The person presents the poster to the class.
   - Listen.
   - Help answer the other students' questions.

LISTENING

A CONVERSATION

1 Work in pairs. Look at the photos. What kind of food can you see?

2 One of the food museums in the world is the Wonderfood Museum in Penang, Malaysia. What do you think you can see in these three parts of the museum?

1 The Info Zone: _____

2 The Wow Zone: _____

3 The Educational Zone: _____

3 🔊 **3.7** You hear a girl called Siti talking to her friend Victor about the Wonderfood Museum. Listen to the first part of their conversation. Are your ideas in Exercise 2 correct?

4 Work in pairs. Compare your answers with a partner. Listen again and check.

5 🔊 **3.8** Listen to the second part of the conversation. Answer the questions.

1 How long is Siti in the museum?
_____ minutes

2 Who is in Siti's favourite photo?
her _____

3 What is one problem with food?
a lot of _____

6 Listen again to the second part of the conversation and check your answers.

ORACY

Showing interest

When someone shows you an interesting photo or tells you something interesting, say something to show you are interested.

7 🔊 **3.9** Can you remember the words that Victor uses to show he's interested? Listen to the whole conversation and write the words he uses.

>>> STRETCH! 🛡 **Digital Literacy** Work in pairs. Go online and find information about the Wonderfood Museum in Penang. What are your favourite photos of the museum? Show other people in your class. Look at other people's favourite photos and show that you are interested!

SELF-ASSESSMENT: UNIT 3

How confident do you feel about:

- talking about food, drink and containers, and using numbers 20–100?
- using *there is / there are*?
- using *some / any / much / many / a lot of*?
- finding new information?
- deciding what information is important?
- answering questions about yourself?
- writing a message?

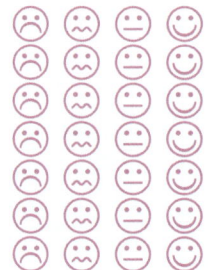

What is your favourite part of Unit 3? Tell your partner.

_____

_____

UNIT 4 GAMES, GAMES, GAMES!

LEARNING AIMS

- **Skills:** talk about abilities and likes / dislikes
- **Grammar:** learn and practise *can* for ability and *like / love / don't like* etc. + *-ing* forms
- **Vocabulary:** learn and practise sports and games verbs and nouns
- **Oracy:** give a presentation
- **Exam practice:** Speaking Part 1, Reading Part 1, Listening Part 5

ORACY

Giving a presentation
- speaking slowly and clearly
- using body language and making eye contact

1 Look at the photo. In pairs, discuss the questions.

1 What sport is this?
2 How do you think the boy feels?

2 Watch the video. Answer the questions.

▶ 01

1 When in life do we start to play?
2 Why are sports important?
3 How many different sports can you think of?

3 Work in pairs. Read the statements below. Take turns to share your opinions.

- Everyone likes sport.
- Watching sport is more fun than playing sport.
- Sport teaches you a lot about life.

4 Think about your discussion. Answer the questions with your partner.

1 Why is it important to speak clearly and at the right pace?
2 Why is it important to use appropriate body language?

Documentary

Grammar

Oracy

| 31

VOCABULARY

SPORTS AND GAMES VERBS

1 🔊 **4.1 Write the verbs under the photos. Listen, check and repeat.**

bounce   catch   hit   jump   kick   ride   run   sail   score   swim   throw   walk

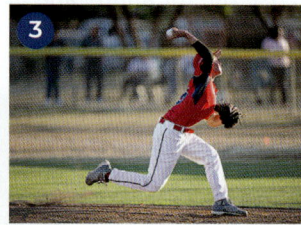

2 Put the verbs from Exercise 1 in the correct column.

Things you do with a ball	Ways of moving
score	

3 Complete the sentences with the verbs from Exercise 1.

1   In lots of sports, you _____ a ball with a bat.
2   You _____ a ball with your foot.
3   Do you know how to _____ a horse?
4   I _____ lots of goals for my football team.
5   When we are on holiday, we _____ in the sea every day.
6   My brother can _____ 60 metres in ten seconds!
7   _____ the ball to me and I'll _____ it.
8   In basketball, you _____ the ball when you run.
9   We love to _____ in our boat.
10 This basketball player isn't tall – but he can _____ very high!

4 Look again at the photos in Exercise 1. What sports and games can you see? Which sports are team sports (sports you can *only* play in teams)?

5 Think back to the video. Which team sports are in the video? Why are they good for you?

6 ▶ **01 Watch the video again and check your answers in Exercise 5.**

ORACY

Speaking slowly and clearly

When you speak, pronounce your words clearly. This helps people understand you.

7 Work in pairs. What other sports can you think of? Use a dictionary if you need to. Then discuss the questions below. Don't forget to pronounce your words clearly!

1   Which is your favourite sport? Why?
2   Which sport do you not like? Why?

🔊 4.2

Skateboard or scooter

– which is best?

Skateboards and scooters are both great. You can ride to school on a skateboard **or** a scooter. You can learn to do amazing tricks on both, too. But which one is best for you? Read and find out.

Learning

1 ____ It takes hours – even days – to learn how to ride a skateboard.

Riding

When you know how to ride a scooter, you can turn corners and stop very easily. 2 ____

Carrying

You can carry a skateboard, no problem at all.
3 ____ Yes, you can – a scooter isn't *hard* to carry, but it's not as easy as a skateboard.

Competition

Skateboarding is an Olympic sport now. You can't win an Olympic gold medal on a scooter!

Cool

Most people think skateboards are cool. Some people think scooters are cool. You choose!

a

b

READING

AN ARTICLE

1 Look at the title of the article and the photos (a–b). Which photo shows a scooter and which one shows a skateboard?

2 Read the article. Put the sentences (a–c) in the correct gaps.

    a On a skateboard those things are quite difficult.

    b Can you carry a scooter?

    c You can learn to ride a scooter in five minutes.

3 Read the article again. Are the sentences true or false?

    1 You can do tricks on a scooter.

    2 It takes a long time to learn how to ride a scooter.

    3 You can turn corners on a scooter.

    4 Scooters are hard to carry.

    5 You can win an Olympic medal on a scooter.

    6 Everyone thinks scooters are cool.

4 Read the title of the article again. What is your answer to the question? Write down your ideas.

ORACY

Giving reasons

When you say what you think, say *why* you think it. Give your reasons!

5 In pairs, talk about which you prefer – skateboard or scooter. Or is there a different way to travel that you like more? Do you agree with each other? Don't forget to say *why* you think something.

>>> STRETCH! Work in pairs. How many different ways can you think of to travel to school? Use a dictionary if you need to. Which pair has the longest list?

GRAMMAR
CAN FOR ABILITY

1 Complete the sentences from the article on page 33.

1 You _____ ride to school on a skateboard or a scooter.

2 _____ you carry a scooter?

3 You _____ win an Olympic medal on a scooter.

2 Choose the correct answers to complete the rules in the grammar box.

> ### can for ability
>
> We use *can / can't* to talk about ability in the present.
> *Can / Can't* go [1] *before / after* verbs.
> She **can** ride a bicycle. He **can't** sail.
> In questions, *can* goes at the [2] *beginning / end*.
> **Can** you ride a bicycle?
>
> ▶ Grammar reference and practice page 101

3 🖳 Go to the digital activities.

4 Are the sentences true or false? Correct the false sentences.

Dogs can catch.

Horses can't jump.

A duck can ride a scooter.

Monkeys can throw.

Snakes can run.

Spiders can't talk.

5 (PRONUNCIATION) Go to the digital pronunciation activity.

6 Write questions and answers.

1 you / ride a skateboard ✓
   Can you ride a skateboard? *Yes, I can.*

2 your teacher / speak English? ✓

3 your dad / cook? ✗

4 you / swim? ✓

5 your parents / play chess? ✗

>>> STRETCH! Work in groups to play Guess Who. On a piece of paper write three things that you *can* do and three things that you *can't* do. Give your paper to another student. That person reads the notes to the group, and they try to guess who it is.

SPEAKING
ANSWERING QUESTIONS ABOUT YOURSELF

1 Work in pairs. Think of three questions about sports. Think of answers to the questions.

> ### EXAM TIP
>
> In Speaking Part 1, the examiner always asks you your name, your age and where you live. Practise answering these questions.

2 🔊 4.3 Read the conversation and put the questions (a–f) in the correct gaps. Then listen and check.

a How old are you?

b Tell me something about the hockey team.

c What's your name?

d What sports or games do you like?

e What sports do you like to watch?

f Where do you live?

Examiner: Hello, I'm Mark. [1] ____

Student: Hello, I'm Alyssa.

Examiner: [2] ____

Student: I'm 12 years old.

Examiner: [3] ____

Student: I live in Córdoba.

Examiner: Now let's talk about sports and games. [4] ____

Student: I like hockey and chess.

Examiner: [5] ____

Student: I like to watch tennis and baseball.

Examiner: What sports do you play at school?

Student: I play in the school hockey team.

Examiner: [6] ____

Student: We play every Tuesday and Friday. We play other school teams. We're a good team.

> ### ☑ EXAM TRAINING   SPEAKING PART 1
>
> **3** Work in pairs. Take turns to ask and answer the questions in Exercise 2.

HOW IS UNIT 4 SO FAR?

☆☆☆ I understand   ☆☆ I'm getting there   ☆ I don't understand

MIND SPORTS

Are you a 'mind sports' player? Maybe you don't know what a mind sport is, but I'm sure that you sometimes play them. Even people who love playing physical sports often like playing mind sports. So, what are they?

There are different kinds of mind sports. Board games like chess and backgammon are mind sports. So are puzzles like Sudoku and Rubik's Cube. Spelling competitions and maths problems are all mind sports, too.

Every year there is a Mind Sports Olympiad in London, England. People come from all over the world to try to win prizes. Some of the best players are only 12.

They also play some unusual games at the Mind Sports Olympiad. For example, in diving chess they play chess underwater in a swimming pool!

Scientists say that mind sports can improve your memory and help you think better. But playing physical sports is good for your body AND your brain. So maybe it is best to play both!

READING

AN ARTICLE

1 Look at the photos in the article. What do these games have in common?

2 Read the article quickly. What is the Mind Sports Olympiad?

3 ◁)) 4.4 Read and listen to the article. Choose the correct answers to complete the sentences.

1 Mind sports are for people who
   A don't like physical sports.
   B enjoy playing games.
2 The Mind Sports Olympiad is
   A an international competition.
   B only for young people.
3 Scientists believe that mind sports are
   A good for your brain.
   B good for your brain and your body.

4 Work in pairs. Which do you like more – mind sports or physical sports? Why?

VOCABULARY

SPORTS AND GAMES NOUNS

1 ◁)) 4.5 Write the words under the photos. Listen, check and repeat.

chess   competition   player   prize   puzzle
roller skates   sports centre   swimming pool

2 Complete the sentences with the correct form of words from Exercise 1.

1 It is difficult to learn how to play
   _____ .
2 We've got a _____ in our garden, but we don't use it in the winter.
3 How many _____ are there in the team?
4 I love doing _____ , but this one is very difficult.
5 You can play lots of sports in the
   _____ .
6 Sienna wants a pair of _____ .
7 The first _____ in this spelling _____ is 100 euros.

GRAMMAR

LIKE, LOVE, DON'T LIKE, ETC. + -ING FORMS

1 Watch the grammar vlog. What sport does Marco like playing? ▶ 02

2 Complete the sentences from the grammar vlog.

1 I love _____ gymnastics.
2 I hate _____ sports.
3 Tina _____ losing.

3 Choose the correct answers to complete the rules in the grammar box.

> **like, love, don't like, etc. + -ing forms**
>
> We use the *-ing* form of the verb after *(not) like / love / don't mind / hate* to say how we feel about an activity.
> He **loves** [1] *swimming / swim*.
> I don't **like** [2] *doing / do* homework.
>
> ▶ Grammar reference and practice page 101

4 Go to the digital activities.

5 Look at the table. Write sentences about Toby and Sara.

	play board games	do puzzles	swim
Toby	😍	🙂	😣
Sara	☹️	🙂	😐
You			

1 Toby / puzzles
   Toby likes doing puzzles.
2 Sara / puzzles
   _____
3 Toby / board games
   _____
4 Sara / swim
   _____
5 Toby / swim
   _____
6 Sara / board games
   _____

6 Complete the table for you. Write sentences.

> **DIGITAL CLASSROOM**
> PRACTICE EXTRA UNIT 4

7 Write five other things that you *love*, *like*, *don't mind*, *don't like* and *hate*. Work in groups and read your list to each other. What do most people agree / disagree about?

READING

REAL-WORLD TEXTS

> **EXAM TIP**
>
> In Reading Part 1, you read short texts. Look at each text and decide what type of text it is.

1 Look at the texts in Exercise 2. What type of text is each one?

> an email   a sign   a text message

> ☑ **EXAM TRAINING** ◁ **READING PART 1**

2 Read the texts. For each question, choose the correct answer.

1
> **Coach**
> Online
>
> Basketball practice is in the playground today (NOT gym).
>
> 3.30 start, as always.   🔊 4.6

A Basketball begins at a different time today.
B Basketball is in a different place today.
C There is no basketball practice today.

2
> Sam,
>
> I've got the tickets for the rugby game this weekend. They are 4 euros each. Please pay me after class.
>
> Thanks, Jo

A Jo wants to play rugby.
B Jo wants to give Sam money.
C Jo wants money from Sam.

3
> # FOR SALE
>
> Scooter – 4 years old
> Perfect condition
> Only 5 euros

A The scooter is like new.
B The scooter is for a child.
C The scooter is difficult to ride.

WRITING

A BLOG POST

1 Read Kenan's blog post. What is the best title?

A Writing a blog

B What I love and hate

C Movies and rock

HOME ⌄   **BLOGS** ⌄   CONTACT ⌄

¹OK, there are lots of blog posts on the web about the unusual things people love and hate, so here's mine. ²Lots of people love going to the cinema, but I don't. ³I hate listening to other people eat and talk in the cinema. ⁴Also, nearly all of my friends hate listening to classical music, but I love it. I hate rock music. ⁵What unusual things do you love and hate?

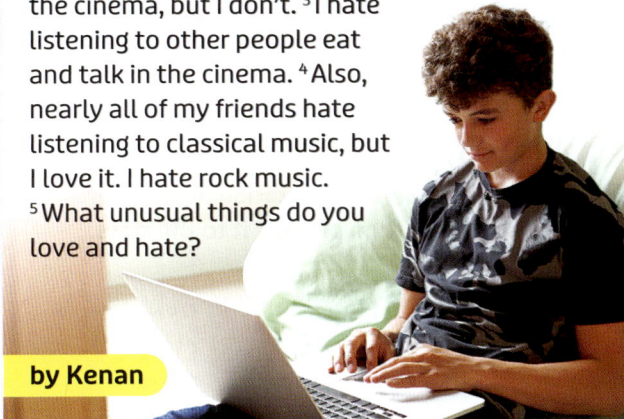

by Kenan

2 Are the sentences true or false? Correct the false sentences.

1 Kenan loves going to the cinema.

2 Kenan's friends hate listening to rock music.

3 Kenan loves listening to classical music.

3 Read the blog post again. In which sentence (1–5) does Kenan do these things?

a Asks a question   5

b Talks about something most people love

c Says why he is writing

d Says why he hates something

e Talks about something most people hate

4 Now write a blog post about things you love and hate. Follow the structure of Kenan's blog post.

5 Read your blog post again and check your work. Use these questions to help you.

1 Do you follow the structure of Kenan's blog post?

2 Do you use the *-ing* form of the verb after *like*, *love*, *hate*, etc.?

3 Is the spelling and grammar correct?

6 Now work in pairs. Read each other's blog posts and give feedback. Use the questions in Exercise 5 to help you. Make a note of your partner's feedback and write a second draft of your blog post.

LISTENING

A CONVERSATION

1 Look at the photos. What sports can you see? Where can you play these sports?

2 🔊 4.7 Look at the exam task in Exercise 3. Listen and read the first part of the phone conversation. What sports do you hear? What is Paco's favourite sport?

Mum: Hi, Paco. How's your day at the sports centre?

Paco: Great. There are so many sports to play, including my favourite!

Mum: Is that badminton? Or tennis?

Paco: I like badminton and tennis, but my favourite now is hockey.

☑ EXAM TRAINING   LISTENING PART 5

EXAM TIP

Don't write any answers the first time you listen. Wait until the second listen before you answer.

3 🔊 4.8 For each question, choose the correct answer.

You will hear Paco talking to his mother on the phone about his friends' activities at the sports centre. Which sport is each person's favourite?

People		Sport	
0	Paco _D_	A	swimming
1	Jacob ____	B	skateboarding
2	Marta ____	C	badminton
		~~D~~	~~hockey~~
		E	tennis

4 🎓 **Emotional Development** Work in groups. Imagine you are in a sports centre. Think about sports you want and don't want to play. Work together to create a sports timetable for the day. Try to make everyone happy!

ORACY

GIVING A PRESENTATION

- speaking slowly and clearly
- using body language and making eye contact

1 Work in pairs. Look at the advice for giving a presentation. There is one piece of bad advice. Can you find it?

a Don't talk too quickly.
b Don't talk too quietly.
c Don't look at people.
d Move your body and arms.
e Stand up straight.

2 Change the bad advice in Exercise 1 into good advice.

3 Watch Daniella practising her presentation. What advice in Exercise 1 does she follow? Complete the table.

	Daniella does this (✓) / (✗)
Don't talk too quickly.	
Don't talk too quietly.	
Move your body and arms.	
Stand up straight.	

4 ▶ 04 Watch the students talking about Daniella's presentation. Do they agree with your answers in Exercise 3?

5 ▶ 05 Now watch Daniella doing her presentation. Is it better? Why? / Why not?

6 Plan and practise a presentation about your favourite sport. Then present it to the class.

Who plays?
How do you play?
When do you play?
My favourite sport
Where do you play?
Why do you like it?

7 Watch everyone give their presentations. Do they follow the advice in Exercise 1?

SELF-ASSESSMENT: UNIT 4

How confident do you feel about:

- talking about sports?
- asking and answering questions about abilities?
- talking about things you like and dislike doing?
- pronouncing words clearly when you speak?
- writing about things you love and hate?
- answering questions about yourself?
- giving a presentation?

What is your favourite part of Unit 4? Tell your partner.

_____
_____

UNIT 5 EVERY DAY'S A NEW DAY!

LEARNING AIMS

- **Skills**: describe and ask about daily routines
- **Grammar**: learn and practise the present simple and adverbs of frequency, and present simple questions
- **Vocabulary**: learn and practise expressions for daily routines, telling the time, and nouns for transport and travel
- **Critical thinking**: think about a new activity you can do every day
- **Exam practice**: Reading Part 2, Speaking Part 2, Listening Part 2

THE CHALLENGE

It's good to do new things!
You will:

- **Stage 1 Think:** think of some new things you want to do.
- **Stage 2 Prepare:** choose one new thing to do for ten minutes every day, and plan how and when to do it.
- **Stage 3 Develop:** make a video presentation about the new activity.
- **Stage 4 Present:** show the video to the class and answer questions about it.

1 Look at the photo. In pairs, discuss the questions.

1 Where is the person?
2 What part of the day is it?

2 Watch the video. Is Mya's day different from your day? How?

▶ 01

CHALLENGE ① ② ③ ④

Think

Work in small groups. Draw a mind map.

1 Draw a mind map to help you think of new things you can do. Think of ideas for these things. If you don't know the words in English, draw pictures or look up the words in a dictionary.

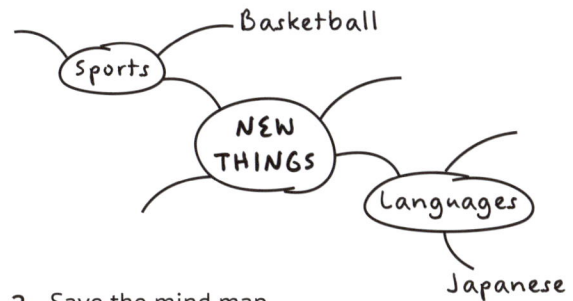

2 Save the mind map.

Documentary

Grammar

VOCABULARY

DAILY ROUTINES

1 🔊 **5.1 Match the words (1–12) to the photos (a–l). Listen, check and repeat.**

1	brush my teeth	4	go to bed	7	have lunch	10	play sports
2	do my homework	5	have a shower	8	have dinner	11	practise dance moves
3	get up	6	have breakfast	9	meet my friends	12	watch a film

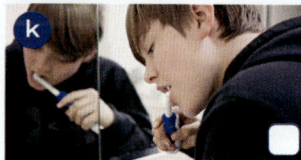

2 ▶ **01 Think back to the video. Which daily routines in Exercise 1 are in the video? Watch again to check.**

3 Complete the sentences with verbs from Exercise 1.

1 I _____ my friends at school.
2 I _____ my teeth two or three times a day.
3 I _____ up early.
4 I _____ my homework after school.
5 I _____ dance moves every day!
6 I _____ to bed late in the holidays.

WHAT'S THE TIME?

4 🔊 **5.2 Write the words in the correct places. Listen, check and repeat.**

half   o'clock   past   quarter

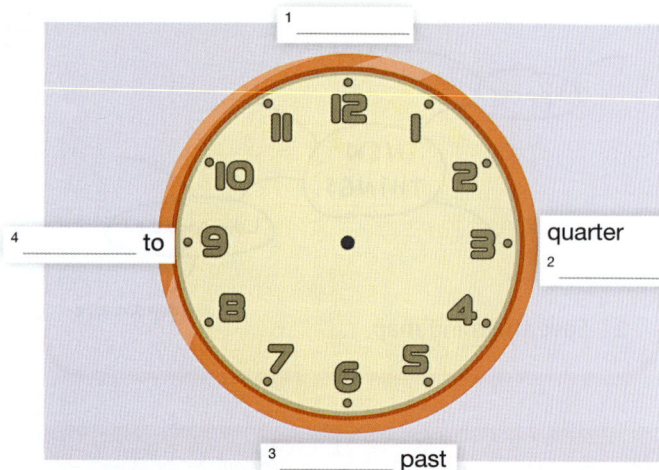

1 _____

4 _____ to   quarter 2 _____

3 _____ past

5 Write three times in numbers (for example, 10.15). In pairs, ask and answer *What's the time?*

6 Write the times in words.

1
It's twenty-five to six.

2 _____

3 _____

4 _____

5 _____

6 _____

7 _____

8 _____

7 Tell your partner about your day, with times. Use the words in Exercise 1.

> I get up at quarter past seven.

READING

SHORT TEXTS

1 Look at the photos. Where are the teenagers?

2 Read the texts quickly. Who does Jordan help after school? Where does Stella live?

MY DAY!

My parents have a café and I often help them after school. My sister and I always have dinner in the café, and we usually watch a film together. I never go to bed before eleven, but I don't get up before half past eight because I live very near my school. Every day, I have a shower, have my breakfast and brush my teeth in 15 minutes!

JORDAN

I'm travelling round the world with my family – on a boat! I get up at six every morning, but I don't have a shower – I have a swim! I have all my school lessons online. I meet my friends online, too, and we practise our dance moves together. That's sometimes difficult for me on the boat! I don't watch many films and I usually go to bed at nine o'clock.

STELLA

3 🔊 5.3 Work in pairs. Read and listen to the texts and complete the table.

	Jordan	Stella
When they get up:		
How often they have a shower:		
When they go to bed:		
How often they watch films:		

4 Look at question 1 in Exercise 5 and the information in Exercise 3. Is the answer A or B? Why?

✓ EXAM TRAINING ◀ READING PART 2

EXAM TIP

Read each question carefully so you know which information to look for. There is usually information about each question in more than one text, but there is only one correct answer.

5 Now look at questions 2–4. For each question, choose the correct answer. Use the information in Exercise 3 to help you.

		Jordan	Stella
1	Who gets up very early?	A	B
2	Who never has a shower?	A	B
3	Who goes to bed late?	A	B
4	Who often watches a film in the evening?	A	B

6 🎓 Critical Thinking Work in groups of four. Follow the instructions.

- Pair A: think about three good things and three bad things about helping in a café after school.
- Pair B: think about three good things and three bad things about living on a boat.
- Then tell each other what you think.

🛡 CHALLENGE ─1─2─3─4

Prepare

1 In your group, look at the mind map from Stage 1.
2 Choose one new thing to do. Can you do it for ten minutes every day?
3 What do you need for this activity? Where can you do it? When can you do it?
4 Make notes for your video presentation.

GRAMMAR

PRESENT SIMPLE AND ADVERBS OF FREQUENCY

1 Watch the grammar vlog. How does Lara go to school? Who does she go with?

▶ 02

2 Look at the examples from the grammar vlog. Complete the rules in the grammar box.

- I *usually* **get up** at half past seven.
- Lucas *sometimes* **gets up** before me.
- I don't *often* **go** to bed late.
- Lucas doesn't *usually* **go** to bed early.

> **Present simple**
>
> **Positive sentences:**
> - We add [1] _____ to the verb after *she/he/it*. If the verb ends in *ss, sh, ch, x* or *z* or a vowel (*a, e, i, o, u*), we add *es*.
>
> **Negative sentences:**
> - We use [2] _____ before the main verb after *I/you/we/they*.
> - We use [3] _____ before the main verb after *she/he/it*.
>
> **Adverbs of frequency** come [4] _____ the main verb.
>
> ▶ Grammar reference and practice page 102

3 🖥 Go to the digital activities.

4 Choose the correct answers.

1 She *don't / doesn't* have a shower before breakfast.
2 *They / He* has lunch at two o'clock.
3 You *don't / doesn't* go to bed late.
4 *We / It* don't live here.
5 We *meet / meets* our friends after school.

5 Complete the sentences with the correct form of the verb in brackets.

1 She _____ (go) to bed at half past nine.
2 He _____ (not have) breakfast at quarter to eight.
3 She _____ (practise) her dance moves in the morning.
4 He _____ (brush) his teeth after dinner.
5 She _____ (not do) her homework with her sister.
6 He _____ (play) sports every day.

6 🖥 **PRONUNCIATION** Go to the digital pronunciation activity.

7 Put the adverbs of frequency in brackets in the correct place in the sentences.

1 She meets her friends at the weekend. (always)
   She always meets her friends at the weekend.
2 I brush my teeth after lunch. (sometimes)
   _____
3 We have dinner with our grandparents. (often)
   _____
4 He doesn't do his homework in the morning. (usually)
   _____
5 They don't watch a film after dinner. (always)
   _____
6 I have a shower in the afternoon. (never)
   _____

ORACY

Asking for people's opinions about your ideas

Remember to ask other students what they think about your ideas. You can say: *Is that a good idea? / What do you think? / Do you agree?* This shows your classmates that their opinions are important. They can answer: *Great! / Good idea! / I'm not sure that's a good idea because ....*

🛡 CHALLENGE — ① ② ③ ④

Develop

1 In your group, choose one or two people to give the presentation and one or two people to make the video.
2 Make some more notes for the presentation. What things do you need for the video: a phone, some pictures of the activity?
3 Make the video together in your group.

HOW IS UNIT 5 SO FAR?

☆☆☆ I understand   ☆☆ I'm getting there   ☆ I don't understand

HOW DO THEY GET TO SCHOOL?

All over the world, people go to school in different ways. A lot of teenagers walk or go on bikes; some parents drive their children to school in a car or on a motorbike; many students take a bus or a train. How do you usually go to school?

In some parts of the world, it's difficult to walk or go on a bike to school. And in some places, there aren't any buses or trains. What do people do in those places?

There's a video online where you can see children in one part of Colombia travelling to school in a very special way: they don't fly in a helicopter or in a plane, but they fly through the air on a zipline. It's very fast! One girl always goes on the zipline with her mother, and one boy goes with his brother.

In some places, students can take cable cars to school. And in places where there's lots of snow, kids drive snowmobiles! In other places, children ride to school on horses. People also go by boat, by lorry or sometimes even by tractor!

The important thing is for all the children to get to school, even if it's sometimes difficult!

READING

AN ARTICLE

1 Work in pairs. Look at the photos. Which are fun ways to go to school?

2 ◁)) **5.4** Read and listen to the article. <u>Underline</u> all the different ways people can travel to school.

3 Read the article again. Choose the correct answers.

1 Do many teenagers walk or go to school on bikes?
Yes, they do. / No, they don't.

2 Do the children in Colombia fly in a helicopter?
Yes, they do. / No, they don't.

3 Does the girl go on the zipline with her mother?
Yes, she does. / No, she doesn't.

4 Does the boy go on the zipline with his father?
Yes, he does. / No, he doesn't.

5 Do some children go to school on horses?
Yes, they do. / No, they don't.

>>> STRETCH! Work in pairs. Look online to find places where people travel to school using the types of transport in the article. Can you find the video about the children in Colombia going to school by zipline?

VOCABULARY

TRANSPORT AND TRAVEL

1 ◁)) **5.5** Find the words for types of transport in the article and write them under the photos. Then listen, check and repeat.

2 Think of a type of transport. Work in pairs and ask and answer questions to find out what it is.

Is it big / fast / expensive / …?

3 🛡 **Creative Thinking** Work in small groups. Think of fun ways for you to get to your school. Draw pictures to show the class!

GRAMMAR

PRESENT SIMPLE QUESTIONS

1 **Complete the questions and answers from the article and Exercise 3 on page 43.**

1 How _____ you usually go to school?
2 What _____ people do in those places?
3 _____ many teenagers walk or go to school on bikes?
4 Yes, they _____ . / No, they _____ .
5 _____ the girl go on the zipline with her mother?
6 Yes, she _____ . / No, she _____ .

2 **Complete the rules with the words in the box.**

> do x2   does x2   doesn't   don't

Present simple questions

- We use [1] _____ for questions with *I/you/we/they.*
  Answers: *Yes, I/you/we/they* [2] _____ ./
  No, I/you/we/they [3] _____ .
- We use [4] _____ for questions with *she/he/it.*
  Answers: *Yes, she/he/it* [5] _____ ./
  No, she/he/it [6] _____ .

▶ Grammar reference and practice page 102

3 📱 **Go to the digital activities.**

4 **Write questions and answers using the present simple.**

1 your brother and sister / do their homework? ✔
  Do your brother and sister do their homework?
  Yes, they do.

2 your sister / often / meet her friends? ✔
  _____

3 you / sometimes / go to bed late? ✔
  _____

4 What time / you / usually / get up?
  _____ 🕖 7:30

5 your parents / play sports? ✗
  _____

6 your brother / usually / go to school on his bike? ✗
  _____

DIGITAL CLASSROOM
PRACTICE EXTRA UNIT 5

ORACY

Taking turns

When you work with a partner, take turns to speak.

> It's your turn.   It's my turn.

5 **Work in pairs. Take turns to ask and answer questions. Use Exercise 4 to help you.**

SPEAKING

TALKING ABOUT YOUR LIKES AND DISLIKES

EXAM TIP

In Speaking Part 2, say what you like or don't like about the activities, things or places in the pictures and give reasons. Ask your partner questions and take turns to speak.

1 **Look at the pictures on page 109. Do you like these activities? Make sentences to give reasons.**

> I like
> I don't like
> cycling
> travelling by car
> walking
> because

> it's fun / difficult.
> I can talk to my friends.
> it's fast / slow.
> I can't play games on my phone.

2 🔊 **5.6 Listen to two students doing part of the Speaking exam. Do both students talk about all three activities? Who gives long answers? Is that good?**

3 **Listen again and answer the questions.**

1 How does Mira go to school? Who does she go with?
2 How does Carlos go to school? Who does he go with?
3 Can you think of some long answers to help Carlos?

☑ EXAM TRAINING **SPEAKING PART 2**

4 **Work in pairs and talk for two minutes about the pictures on page 108. Do you like these different activities? Say why or why not.**

A SOCIAL MEDIA POST

1 Look at Cameron's holiday photos. Where do you think Cameron is on holiday? What kind of holidays do you like? Why?

2 Read Cameron's social media post. What does Cameron like about being on holiday?

Cameron
@Cams14 · Follow

Hey everyone!

I love it here! All my days are so different from my normal school days! I never get up before ten o'clock 😎 and after a big breakfast, I usually meet my friends for a swim. In the afternoon, we often play table tennis or football and fly our kites on the beach.

Are any of you on holiday right now? Tell me about your days!

3 Read the social media post again. Are the sentences true or false?

1 Cameron gets up early on holiday.
2 Cameron often goes swimming before breakfast.
3 Cameron plays sports after lunch.

4 Work in pairs. Imagine you're on holiday. Make notes about three things you do.

5 Write a reply to Cameron's post. Use your notes from Exercise 4 and use some of the language from this unit. Write 35–70 words.

6 Read your social media post again and check your work. Use these questions to help you.

1 Does your post talk about three things you do on holiday?
2 Are there words from this unit in your post?
3 Is the spelling and grammar correct?

7 Now work in pairs. Read each other's social media posts and give feedback. Use the questions in Exercise 6 to help you. Make a note of your partner's feedback and write a second draft of your post.

8 🛡 Critical Thinking Work in groups. Discuss the questions.

1 Do you like doing new activities?
2 Why is it good to sometimes do new activities?
3 Is it good to do new activities when you're on holiday? Why? / Why not?

>> STRETCH! Work in pairs. Role play a video call with a friend on holiday. Ask each other questions about your days.

CHALLENGE 1 2 3 4

Present

1 Present your video to the class.
2 Answer your classmates' questions.

LISTENING

A MONOLOGUE

1 Work in pairs. Do you listen to podcasts? What kind of podcasts do you like?

2 🔊 **5.7** Work in pairs. Look at the photos. Where do you think the island is? Listen to the beginning of Kayla's podcast to find out.

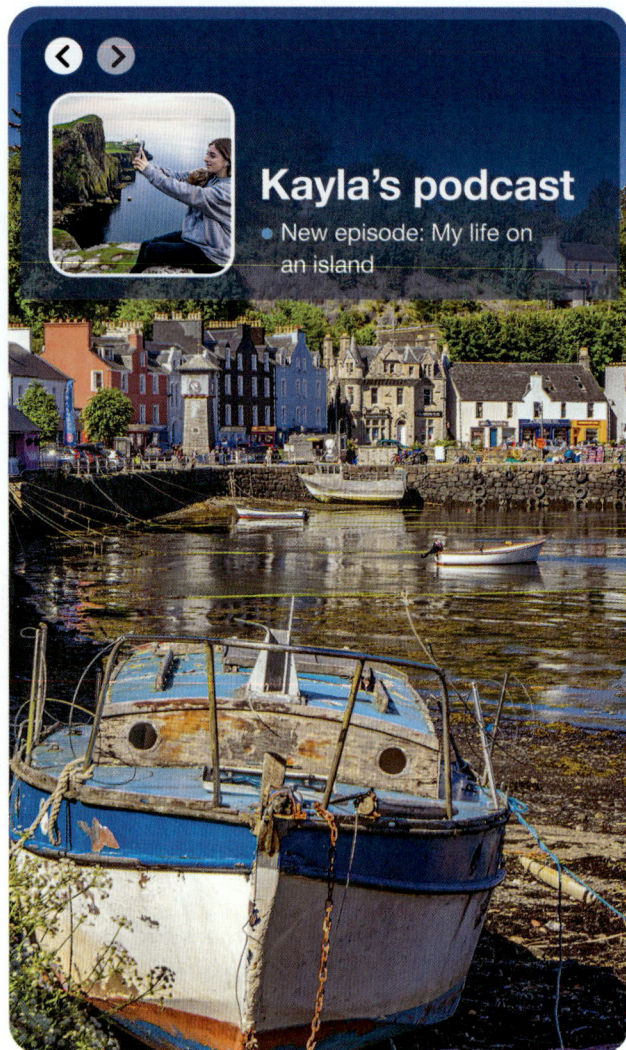

Kayla's podcast
● New episode: My life on an island

3 Look at the exam task in Exercise 4. Where do you need to write these things?

- a type of transport
- what the island is called
- a time

☑ EXAM TRAINING LISTENING PART 2

EXAM TIP

You always hear the information in the same order as it is in the notes.

4 🔊 **5.8** For each question, write the correct answer in the gap. Write one word or a number or a date or a time.

You will hear a girl called Kayla talking about her life on an island.

My life on an island

Number of people on island:	(0)	_3,000_
Name of island:	(1)	_____
Kayla gets up at:	(2)	_____ am
How Kayla travels to school:	by (3)	_____

5 Listen to Kayla's podcast again and check your answers.

6 🅖 **Critical Thinking** Work in pairs. Find out about the island of Mull. Do you think it is a good place to live? Why? / Why not? (Think about the weather, friends, school and activities you can do.)

⟫⟫ STRETCH! Work in pairs. Make a podcast about your days. Take turns to talk about your lives. Play the podcast to your class.

SELF-ASSESSMENT: UNIT 5

How confident do you feel about:

- talking about your days and other people's days?
- telling the time?
- using adverbs of frequency?
- asking and answering questions using the present simple?
- asking for and giving opinions about ideas?
- talking about transport and travel?
- taking turns to speak?

What is your favourite part of Unit 5? Tell your partner.

_____
_____

CONTENTS

GRAMMAR REFERENCE AND PRACTICE

STEAM INVESTIGATIONS

SCIENCE

Why are we all different?

Nature + nurture = YOU!

You are who you are because of your **genes** (nature), and also because of your **environment** (nurture). These two factors work together to determine everything about you. For example, your **biological parents'** height affects how tall you are, but getting enough food to eat can also have some **influence**. We can use a Venn diagram to show characteristics.

Nature
Your biological mother's genes + Your biological father's genes

Nurture
What you eat

A Venn diagram showing how 'nature' and 'nurture' affect us

① THINK

- List three ways you are different from your friends.
- List three ways you are the same as your friends.
- In your opinion, why are people different?

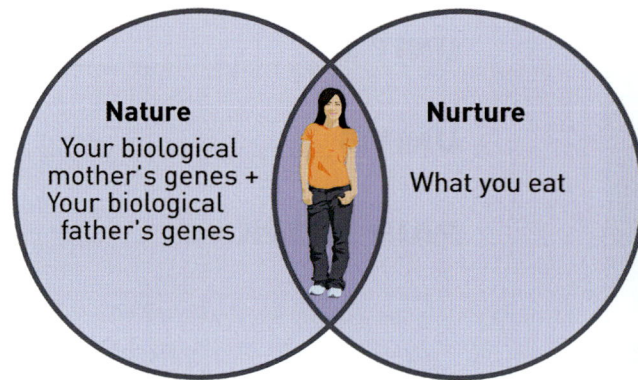

④ INVESTIGATE:
What makes me 'me'?

🔍 RESEARCH

1.1 Work individually.

1.2 Make a list of eight facts about yourself, e.g., what you like doing, what you are good at, what you look like, what you like to eat.

1.3 Think: in your opinion, are these facts because of nature, nurture or both?

✏️ CREATE

2.1 Draw a Venn diagram like the one in the text.

2.2 Write your facts into the correct area in the Venn diagram.

2.3 Draw a picture to represent each fact.

You have genes in the nucleus of all your **cells**. You **inherit** half from your mother and half from your father. This partly explains why biological brothers and sisters often look similar but are not exactly the same: they have some genes which are the same and some which are different. Identical twins have the same genetic information, so look very similar.

Genes are made from DNA. Your environment can make your cells 'activate' or 'deactivate' certain genes. This changes how your body works.

DNA is found in the nucleus of cells

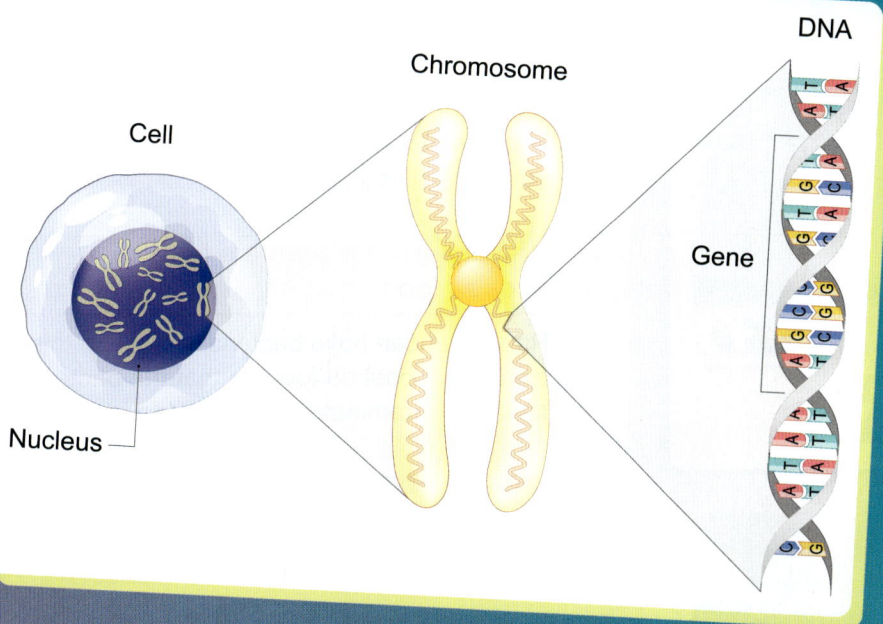

Cell
Nucleus
Chromosome
DNA
Gene

③ EXPLORE

For each of the statements below, decide if you think they are because of nature, nurture or both.

1 Laura's family speak Spanish at home. Laura speaks Spanish and English at school.
2 Xiaoriu has black hair. Her brother has black hair, too.
3 Sammy works hard in maths class. He does well in his maths test.
4 Jean likes football. His sister likes swimming.
5 Samina writes with her left hand. Her mother also writes with her left hand.

Think of one more characteristic that might be controlled by genes and one that might be controlled by environment. Share your ideas with your classmates.

Glossary

biological parent (n) a mother or father of a person or an animal who provides their genetic information

cell (n) the smallest basic unit of a plant or animal

environment (n) the land where people live, and the people they interact with

gene (n) a part of the DNA that controls what you inherit from your parents, e.g., eye colour, hair colour, etc.

influence (n) the power to have an effect on people or things

inherit (v) to be born with the same physical or mental characteristics as one of your parents or grandparents

🖥 PRESENT ➔ 💬 REFLECT

3.1 Get into a group of three.

3.2 Present your Venn diagram to the people in your group.

3.3 Look at your classmates' diagrams. Are they the same as yours? Discuss.

4.1 After your discussion, add one more fact to your Venn diagram.

4.2 Is your Venn diagram clear?

4.3 Do the pictures help your classmates understand your Venn diagram?

STEAM INVESTIGATIONS

SCIENCE

How can I cook safely?

① THINK

Look at the picture of the kitchen.

- Is the kitchen clean or dirty?
- Make a list of three problems you can see.
- Share your list with a classmate.

② ENGAGE

SAFETY RULES — in the — KITCHEN

We all like different foods. Some meals are easy to cook and some are more difficult. We need to cook all of them **safely**. Some rules for this are:

a) Wash your hands.

Wash your hands with soap and water to eliminate dirt and to kill bacteria. If you **cough** or **sneeze**, wash your hands again.

b) Keep the kitchen tidy.

You need to tidy the kitchen to make sure you don't hurt yourself.

c) Keep **raw** meat separate from cooked food.

Raw meat can have bacteria in it. Keep this away from cooked food so that the bacteria cannot contaminate the cooked food.

④ INVESTIGATE:

How can I make a sandwich safely?

🔍 RESEARCH

1.1 Work in pairs or groups of three. Choose ingredients for your sandwich.

1.2 Write a list of the ingredients and equipment you will need.

1.3 Discuss the food safety rules you will need to follow.

✏️ CREATE

2.1 Plan how to make your sandwich. Think about all the steps: before, during and after.

2.2 Draw a flow chart on a poster showing all the steps in order.

2.3 Include a picture of your sandwich on your poster.

d) Chop meat and salad on different chopping boards.

A dirty chopping board can contaminate your salad with bacteria.

e) Store food properly.

You need to keep some foods cold in a fridge or a freezer, but you can keep other foods in a cupboard. You can store some foods for a long time, for example baked beans in a tin, but some food will **go rotten** quickly.

f) Ask for help.

If you are not sure, ask an adult. It is important to ask for help if you are not sure how to stay safe.

(3) **EXPLORE**

Read the text. Match the problems (1–5) to the rules in the text (a–f). There is one rule you do not need to use.

1   Meat and salad are together on the same chopping board.
2   Dirty hands.
3   The kitchen is a mess.
4   Raw and cooked meat are together on the worktop.
5   Fresh milk is in a cupboard.

Look at the rule you didn't use. Write a problem. Share your problem with a partner.

Glossary

chop (v) to cut something into pieces with an axe, knife or other sharp instrument

cough (v) to force air out of your lungs through your throat with a short, loud sound

go rotten (v) to become decayed

raw (adj) not cooked

safely (adv) doing things in a way that is not dangerous or puts you at risk

sneeze (v) to send air out from the nose and mouth in an explosive way that you cannot control

PRESENT

3.1   Present your poster to another group.

3.2   Tell them the necessary steps to make your sandwich safely.

REFLECT

4.1   Write down one good thing about your poster.

4.2   Write down one thing to improve.

GRAMMAR REFERENCE AND PRACTICE

UNIT 1

QUESTION WORDS

Question word	Asks about ...	Example
Who?	a person	Rachel, my sister
Where?	a place	New York, England, the cinema, school
When?	a time / day	Sunday, five o'clock, now
What?	a thing	tennis, a bag, films
How often?	a frequency	every Tuesday, sometimes

1 Write the question word *who, where, when, what* or *how often*.

1 _____ ? A party!
2 _____ ? At my house.
3 _____ ? On January 10th.
4 _____ ? Maria, Jack, Silvia, Ben and Tony.
5 _____ ? Every year!

POSSESSIVE ADJECTIVES

	Person	Possessive adjective
Singular	I	my
	you	your
	he	his
	she	her
	it	its
Plural	we	our
	you	your
	they	their

2 Complete the sentences with the correct possessive adjectives.

1 Hello! What's _____ name?
2 That's my sister. _____ name is Paola.
3 Chris and Rowan are British but _____ parents are South African.
4 Maria and I are in the same class. _____ teacher is Mr Wilson.
5 This is a great restaurant! _____ name is Maison Camille.

PRESENT SIMPLE: *BE*

Positive (+)

I **am** = I**'m**	I**'m** from Australia.
You **are** = You**'re**	You**'re** English.
He **is** = He**'s**	He**'s** my brother.
She **is** = She**'s**	She**'s** my sister.
It **is** = It**'s**	It**'s** my camera.
We **are** = We**'re**	We**'re** from Brazil.
They **are** = They**'re**	They**'re** Greek.

Negative (−)

I **am not** = I**'m not**	I**'m not** Italian.
You **are not** = You **aren't**	You **aren't** French.
He **is not** = He **isn't**	He **isn't** my teacher.
She **is not** = She **isn't**	She **isn't** Spanish.
It **is not** = It **isn't**	It **isn't** your book.
We **are not** = We **aren't**	We **aren't** American.
They **are not** = They **aren't**	They **aren't** English.

3 Complete the sentences with the positive form of *be*.

1 My name _____ James.
2 I _____ a doctor.
3 We _____ students.
4 They _____ from Italy.
5 The sky _____ blue.
6 The books _____ on the table.
7 You _____ my best friend.
8 It _____ my birthday today.

4 Complete the sentences with a pronoun and the positive or negative form of *be*.

1 I'm Stefanos and this is Daska. We're Greek; _____ Spanish.
2 Michael is my brother; _____ my friend.
3 Hello, my name's Mr Green. _____ your new English teacher.
4 Look at my new guitar. _____ so cool!
5 Sorry, _____ in this class. You're in room 5.
6 My mum is English. _____ Scottish.
7 _____ in Class 7B with you. I'm in Class 7A.
8 This is your book. _____ my book.

UNIT 2

THIS, THAT, THESE, THOSE

We use *this* (singular) and *these* (plural) to talk about things that are here or near to us.

We use *that* (singular) and *those* (plural) to talk about things that are there or not near to us.

| This pencil is red. | These pencils are orange. | That book is green. | Those books are blue. |

1 Complete the sentences with *this*, *that*, *these* or *those*.

_____ desk is brown.

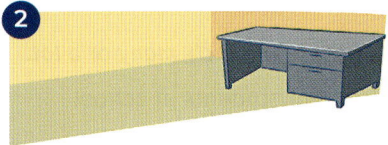
_____ desk is grey.

_____ pens are black.

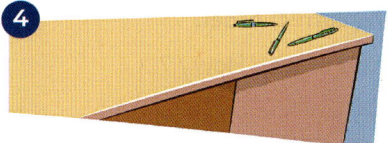
_____ pens are green.

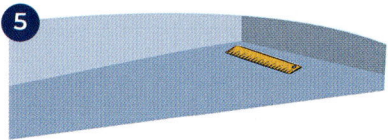
_____ ruler is orange.

_____ ruler is yellow.

POSSESSIVE 'S

This is my mum's cat. It is her cat.
Not ~~This is the cat of my mum~~.

When more than one person share possession, only the last person in the list has 's.

This is Jake and Nat's dog. It is their dog.
Not ~~This is the dog of Jake and Nat~~.

2 Look at the picture and complete the sentences with the correct names and 's.

1 Sally is _____ , _____ and _____ mother.
2 Nat is _____ and _____ son and _____ and _____ brother.
3 Jason is _____ , _____ and _____ father.
4 Katie is _____ and _____ sister and _____ and _____ daughter.
5 Sally is _____ wife.
6 Jason is _____ husband.

HAVE(N'T) GOT

Positive (+)

I/You/We/They**'ve got** a big family.
He/She/It**'s got** two sisters.

Negative (−)

I/You/We/They **haven't got** a new bike.
He/She/It **hasn't got** a brother.

Questions	Short answers
Have you **got** a sister?	Yes, I **have**. / No, I **haven't**.
Has he **got** a piano?	Yes, he **has**. / No, he **hasn't**.

3 Match the questions to the answers.

1 Has Sally got a pet?
2 Have you got a drink?
3 Has Andrew got a smartphone?
4 Have we got the chocolate?
5 Have I got your telephone number?
6 Have you got your keys?

a Yes, he has. It's in his school bag.
b Yes, we have. Here it is!
c No, you haven't. It's 939 405 372.
d Yes, she has. She's got a dog.
e Yes, I have. They're in my coat.
f No, I haven't. I'm thirsty.

UNIT 3

COUNTABLE / UNCOUNTABLE NOUNS, *THERE IS / ARE, THERE ISN'T / AREN'T*

There is (There isn't) - Singular and uncountable
There is a table in the kitchen.
There is some soup.
There isn't an apple.
There isn't any chocolate.

There are (There aren't) - Plural
There are two tables in the kitchen.
There are some eggs.
There aren't any strawberries.

1 Write *there is / are / isn't / aren't*.

1 _____ any bananas. ✗
2 _____ some apples. ✓
3 _____ an egg. ✓
4 _____ any vegetables. ✗
5 _____ a sandwich. ✗
6 _____ some bread. ✓
7 _____ any soup. ✗
8 _____ a bowl. ✗

2 Choose the correct answers.

1 There is *any / an* orange.
2 There isn't *any / a* juice.
3 There are *some / a* plates.
4 There isn't *any / a* bottle.
5 There aren't *some / any* noodles.
6 There is *some / any* salad.
7 There are *a / two* milkshakes.
8 There isn't *any / a* soup.

3 Complete the text with *a, an, some or any*.

Lara brings her lunch to school every day. There's
¹ _____ sandwich in her lunchbox today. She
always has ² _____ cheese in her sandwich.
There is also ³ _____ yoghurt. There isn't
⁴ _____ fruit, but there are ⁵ _____ cakes.
Fraser gets lunch at the canteen. Today there is
⁶ _____ bowl of soup. Or there are ⁷ _____
noodles. There aren't ⁸ _____ cakes at the
canteen. But there ⁹ _____ a lot of fruit. Today
he has ¹⁰ _____ strawberries.

IS THERE / ARE THERE QUESTIONS, *MUCH, MANY, A LOT (OF)*

Questions	Answers
Is there a glass of water?	Yes, **there is.** /
Is there any juice?	No, **there isn't.**
Are there any strawberries?	Yes, **there are.** / No, **there aren't.**
How much fruit **is there** at home?	**There is a lot.** / **There isn't much.**
How many bananas **are there**?	**There are a lot.** / **There aren't many.**

4 Complete the questions with *is there* or *are there*.

1 _____ any fruit juice?
2 _____ an apple in the fridge?
3 _____ any bananas in the kitchen?
4 How many strawberries _____ ?
5 _____ any cakes in the supermarket?
6 How much sugar _____ ?

5 Complete the sentences with *much, many* or *a lot*.

1 There are _____ of students at school today.
2 There isn't _____ cheese in the fridge.
3 There aren't _____ vegetables at home.
4 There isn't _____ bread in the cupboard.
5 There aren't _____ bottles in the kitchen.
6 There is _____ of chocolate in this recipe.

6 Put the words in the correct order.

1 bread / is / there / much / How / ?
_____
2 there / eggs / Are / any / ?
_____
3 There / grapes / many / aren't / .
_____
4 lot / pasta / There / of / a / is / .
_____
5 many / are / tomatoes / there / How / ?
_____
6 much / There / milk / isn't / .
_____

UNIT 4

CAN FOR ABILITY

Positive (+)	Negative (−)
I **can** dance.	I **can't** sing.
You **can** dance.	You **can't** sing.
He/She/It **can** dance.	He/She/It **can't** sing.
We **can** dance.	We **can't** sing.
They **can** dance.	They **can't** sing.
Questions	**Short answers**
Can I cook?	Yes, you **can**. / No, you **can't**.
Can you cook?	Yes, I **can**. / No, I **can't**.
Can he cook?	Yes, he **can**. / No, he **can't**.
	Yes, we **can**. / No, we **can't**.
Can we cook?	Yes, they **can**. / No, they **can't**.
Can they cook?	

1 Complete the sentences with *can* or *can't*.

1 Rose _____ speak Russian well. ✓
2 Thomas _____ take very good photos with his phone. ✗
3 We _____ play the guitar. ✗
4 Jane and Roberta _____ paint pictures very well. ✓
5 My mum _____ sing. ✗
6 I _____ ride a horse. ✓

2 Write the questions and short answers.

1 they / paint pictures?
_____
Yes, _____ .
2 you / ride a horse?
_____
No, _____ .
3 your sister / take good photos?
_____
Yes, _____ .
4 Lizzy and Rita / swim underwater?
_____
No, _____ .
5 you and Martha / play the guitar?
_____
Yes, _____ .
6 Lucca / speak Chinese?
_____
No, _____ .

LIKE, LOVE, DON'T LIKE, ETC. +-ING FORMS

😍 He loves dancing.
🙂 He likes dancing.
😐 He doesn't mind dancing.
🙁 He doesn't like dancing.
😫 He hates dancing.

3 Complete the sentences with *like / likes, don't like / doesn't like*, etc., and the correct form of the verb in brackets.

1 I _____ (play) basketball. 😐
2 Jo _____ (dance). 🙂
3 We _____ (eat) chocolate. 😍
4 Ash _____ (play) football. 🙁
5 Dan and Megan _____ (swim). 😫
6 They _____ (watch) TV every day. 🙁
7 She _____ (be) vegetarian. 😍
8 My dad _____ (cook). 🙂

4 Write sentences with the correct form of the verbs.

1 I / like / read / comics
_____
2 My brother / not like / swim
_____
3 My parents / hate / watch / horror films
_____
4 I / love / play / basketball
_____
5 My friend / not mind / do / homework
_____
6 Harry / hate / get up early / on Saturday
_____
7 I / not like / swim
_____
8 They / not mind / walk / to school
_____

5 Complete the sentences with *like / likes, don't like / doesn't like*, etc., and the correct form of the verb in brackets to make true sentences.

1 I _____ (do) homework.
2 My dad _____ (cook).
3 My mum _____ (drive).
4 My friends _____ (swim).
5 My friends and I _____ (go) to the cinema.
6 My brother / sister / best friend _____ (play) chess.
7 My grandma / grandpa _____ (eat) noodles.
8 I _____ (watch) films in English.

UNIT 5

PRESENT SIMPLE AND ADVERBS OF FREQUENCY

Positive (+)	Negative (–)
I **work** a lot.	I **don't work** a lot.
You **work** a lot.	You **don't work** a lot.
He/She/It **works** a lot.	He/She/It **doesn't work** a lot.
We **work** a lot.	We **don't work** a lot.
They **work** a lot.	They **don't work** a lot.

Adverbs of frequency (*always*, *often*, *usually*, *sometimes*, *never*) go:

- before most verbs.
  You **always take** your phone to school.
  Jane **sometimes does** her homework in bed.
- after the verb *be*.
  We **are never** late for school.
  I **am often** sad on Sunday evenings.

1 Complete the sentences with the present simple form of the verb in brackets.

1 Jack _____ (wake up) at 6.30 am.
2 We _____ (clean) our teeth in the morning and the evening.
3 They _____ (get up) at seven o'clock.
4 I _____ (wash) my face in the morning.
5 Fiona _____ (have) a big breakfast.

2 Write the sentences in Exercise 1 in the negative form.

1 _____
2 _____
3 _____
4 _____
5 _____

3 Write the sentences with the adverb in the correct place.

1 Katia is late for school. (never)
  _____

2 We go to the cinema on Monday evenings. (usually)
  _____

3 I play with my friends at the weekends. (sometimes)
  _____

4 They are at school from Monday to Friday. (always)
  _____

5 Joe likes making cakes. (often)
  _____

PRESENT SIMPLE QUESTIONS

Questions (?)	Short answers
Do I **need** to walk to school?	Yes, you **do**. / No, you **don't**.
Do you **use** IT in English lessons?	Yes, I **do**. / No, I **don't**.
Does she **go** to school on Saturdays?	Yes, she **does**. / No, she **doesn't**.
Do we **have** history on Wednesdays?	Yes, we **do**. / No, we **don't**.
Do they **speak** French?	Yes, they **do**. / No, they **don't**.

4 Complete the present simple questions. Use *do* or *does* and the verb in brackets.

1 _____ he _____ (go) to school by bus?
2 _____ they _____ (study) English in the evening?
3 _____ Sarah _____ (wash) the dishes after dinner?
4 _____ we _____ (go) to the park on Sundays?
5 _____ the cat _____ (play) in the garden?
6 _____ you _____ (do) your homework every day?
7 _____ her parents _____ (drink) coffee in the morning?
8 _____ the bus _____ (leave) at 9 o'clock?

5 Write the questions and short answers.

1 your friends / go / school / by car?
  _____
  (✗) _____
2 Mr Harvey / teach / English?
  _____
  (✓) _____
3 Tony / play / computer games / in the evening?
  _____
  (✗) _____
4 you / have / PE / on Mondays?
  _____
  (✓) _____
5 Maria's dad / watch / a lot / TV?
  _____
  (✓) _____

This page is intentionally blank.

UNIT 5 SPEAKING

PAGE 44, EXERCISE 4

Do you like these different activities?

A

This page is intentionally blank.

CAMBRIDGE

Shining Lights

Workbook **STARTER**

Combo A

A1

Emma Heyderman

This page is intentionally blank.

CONTENTS

UNIT 1 WE'RE ALL DIFFERENT!

VOCABULARY

FAVOURITE THINGS AND ACTIVITIES

1 Find eight things and activities in the word snake.

filmbikecinemacomicbookband boardgameonlinegamingguitar

2 Look at the photos and complete the words.

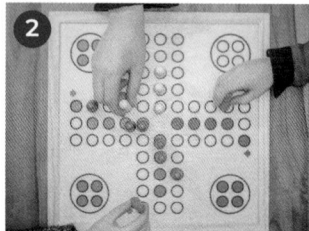

cam_____   boa____ g_____   b_____   gui___ ___ ___

pa___ ___   b___ ___ ___   co___ ___ b___ ___ ___   cin___ ___ ___

3 Match the activities to the photos (1–3) in Exercise 4.

a hiking _____
b swimming _____
c cycling _____

EXAM TIP

Read the text first, <u>before</u> you choose the correct answers.

4 Read the text in the exam task quickly. Tick (✓) the photo of Sophie.

☑ **EXAM TRAINING**   READING PART 4

5 Read the text again. For each question, choose the correct answer.

Meet Sophie Bloom – an important sportsperson!

There's a ¹ _____ about Sophie Bloom. She is a sportsperson and her sport is swimming. She is also a student at university and music is her hobby. She plays the ² _____ and she writes music too. She plays in a ³ _____ with her best friends. The name of their group is Star – it's popular on the internet.

1 A hiking   B camera   C film
2 A party   B guitar   C cinema
3 A bike   B book   C band

NUMBERS 0–20

6 Complete the sums with numbers. Then write all the numbers in words.

1   17 – 10 = _7_   *Seventeen – ten = seven*
2   2 + 11 = ____   _____
3   20 – 8 = ____   _____
4   5 x 3 = ____   _____
5   18 ÷ 2 = ____   _____
6   (19 + 1) – 16 = ____   _____

READING

1 Look at the photo of Beom-seok in the text. How old is he? Guess.

2 Read the first part of the text. Is your answer in Exercise 1 correct?

3 Now read the complete text. Tick (✓) Beom-seok's favourite things and activities.

1   Korean bands   ☐
2   cycling   ☐
3   films   ☐
4   hiking   ☐
5   online gaming ☐
6   parties   ☐

4 Answer the questions. Then read the text again and check your answers.

1   Is Busan a small city in South Korea?
_____

2   What's Beom-seok's favourite music?
_____

3   What's his favourite band?
_____

4   Who is a famous Korean guitar player?
_____

5   What's Beom-seok's family's favourite activity?
_____

YOUR WORLD   🔍   LOG IN

MEET OUR READERS: BEOM-SEOK

Hi Beom-seok! How are you?
Hi! I'm fine, thanks.

Where are you from?
I live in Busan. It's a big city in my country, South Korea, but Seoul is the capital.
Cool! How old are you? **And what's your favourite music?**
I'm 12. My favourite music is K-Pop. That's pop music from Korea.

Is your favourite band BTS?
No, it isn't. I like BTS but my favourite band is Blackpink. I also like Sungha Jung. He plays the guitar, and his videos are very famous.

And your favourite sport is hiking, right?
Yes, it is! In my family we all love hiking in the mountains around the city.

Thanks a lot, Beom-seok. Very interesting!

If you'd like to be in our magazine, send us some interesting answers!

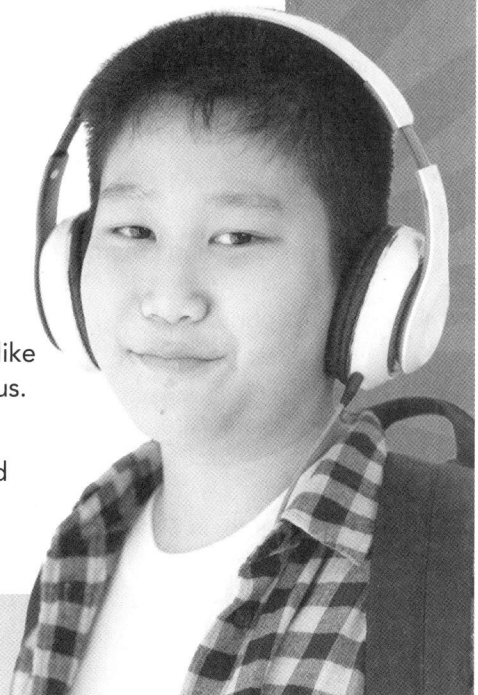

---

5 🧠 Creative Thinking   Would you like to be in the magazine? Write some interesting answers to the questions in the interview.

GRAMMAR

QUESTION WORDS

1 Complete the conversation with the words in the box.

> how   what   where   who   why

A: Hi! ¹ _____'s your name?

B: Hello! I'm Ava.

A: ² _____ are you from?

B: I'm from Cape Town, in South Africa.

A: ³ _____ old are you?

B: I'm 12.

A: ⁴ _____'s your favourite sportsperson?

B: Noko Matlu. She plays football.

A: ⁵ _____ do you like her?

B: Because she's a great player!

POSSESSIVE ADJECTIVES

2 Complete the table with the words in the box.

> his   its   my   she   their   we   you

	Subject pronoun	Possessive adjective
1	I	_____
2	_____	your
3	he	_____
4	_____	her
5	it	_____
6	_____	our
7	they	_____

3 Complete the text with possessive adjectives.

Hi! ¹ _____ name's Leah and I'm from Canada. ² _____ friend is in the photo too. ³ _____ name is Claire. We like reading – ⁴ _____ favourite books are comic books. My brother likes films and ⁵ _____ favourite actor is Timothée Chalamet. What about you? Who's ⁶ _____ favourite actor?

PRESENT SIMPLE: *BE*

4 Choose the correct words to complete the sentences.

1 I *'m not / isn't / aren't* from here. I *'m / 's / 're* from Italy.

2 My teacher *am / is / are* at home. She *'m not / isn't / aren't* at school.

3 Board games *am / is / are* fun! They *'m not / isn't / aren't* boring.

4 Where *am / is / are* you now? *Am / Is / Are* your brother with you?

5 We *'m / 's / 're* 13 years old. How old *am / is / are* your friends?

5 Complete the sentences with the correct form of *be*.

1 My favourite colour _____ red. It _____ blue.

2 My mum _____ with our dog. His name _____ Chips.

3 Where _____ the students? They _____ here!

4 I _____ with my friends, and we _____ at our favourite place!

6 ⟫⟫ STRETCH! **Put the words in the correct order. Then write your answers to the questions.**

1 you / Where / now / are / ?

_____

2 your name / Is / Sam / ?

_____

3 16 / you / Are / ?

_____

4 your / What / favourite / colour / is / ?

_____

5 sportsperson / Who / your / is / favourite / ?

_____

VOCABULARY

DESCRIBING THINGS

1 Choose the correct word for each picture.

cheap / expensive

cheap / expensive

slow / fast

slow / fast

small / big

small / big

2 Complete the adjectives with *a*, *e*, *i*, *o* and *u*.

1 Read this email from your teacher. It's very __mp__rt__nt.
2 I like playing board games with my friends. It's f__n.
3 Is it €20 to see a film in the cinema? That's very __xp__ns__v__.
4 That's a cool hat! Is it n__w?
5 I love this photo. It's b__ __ __t__f__l.

3 🛡 Creative Thinking **Think of things and people to match the descriptions. Use your own ideas.**

1 It's big and expensive.
2 It isn't new. It's very old.
3 They're small and they're cheap.
4 This person is fun.
5 This person is very important to me.

WRITING

AN EMAIL

1 Read Alex's email and write her answers.

	Alex's answers	My answers
1 Name:	Alex	
2 Age:		
3 Country:		
4 Favourite activity:		
5 Best friend:		

< Inbox   2 Messages   ∧ ∨

Hi!

My name's Alex and I'm 13 years old. I'm from Ireland. Our house is in a beautiful town. I love cycling with my family. It's great fun! My favourite person is my best friend, Kian. He's cool!

What are your favourite things?

Write soon,

Alex

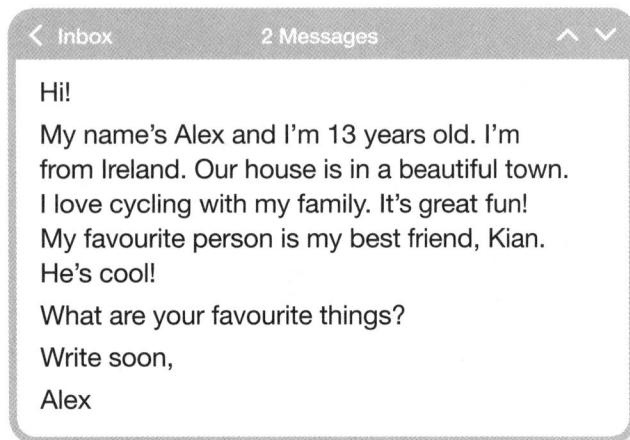

2 Complete the table in Exercise 1 with your answers.

EXAM TIP

First, make notes on the task. Then write your answer.

☑ EXAM TRAINING WRITING PART 6

3 You have a new online friend called Chris Write an email to Chris.

> Say:
> - who you are (name, age and country).
> - what you like.
> - who your best friend is.
>
> Write **20 words** or more.

LISTENING

A CONVERSATION

☑ EXAM TRAINING LISTENING PART 3

EXAM TIP

First, read and listen to the instructions. Who will you hear?

1 ◁) **1.01 Read and listen to the instructions. Who will you hear?**

> For each question, choose the correct answer.
>
> You will hear Gari talking to his friend Lola about his favourite thing.

2 Now read questions 1 and 2 and <u>underline</u> the important words.

> 1 Gari's bike is
> A big.
> B beautiful.
> C old.
>
> 2 What is Gari's favourite thing?
> A online gaming
> B board games
> C games at parties

3 ◁) **1.02 Listen to the conversation. For each question in Exercise 2, choose the correct answer.**

4 ◁) **1.02 Listen again and check your answers.**

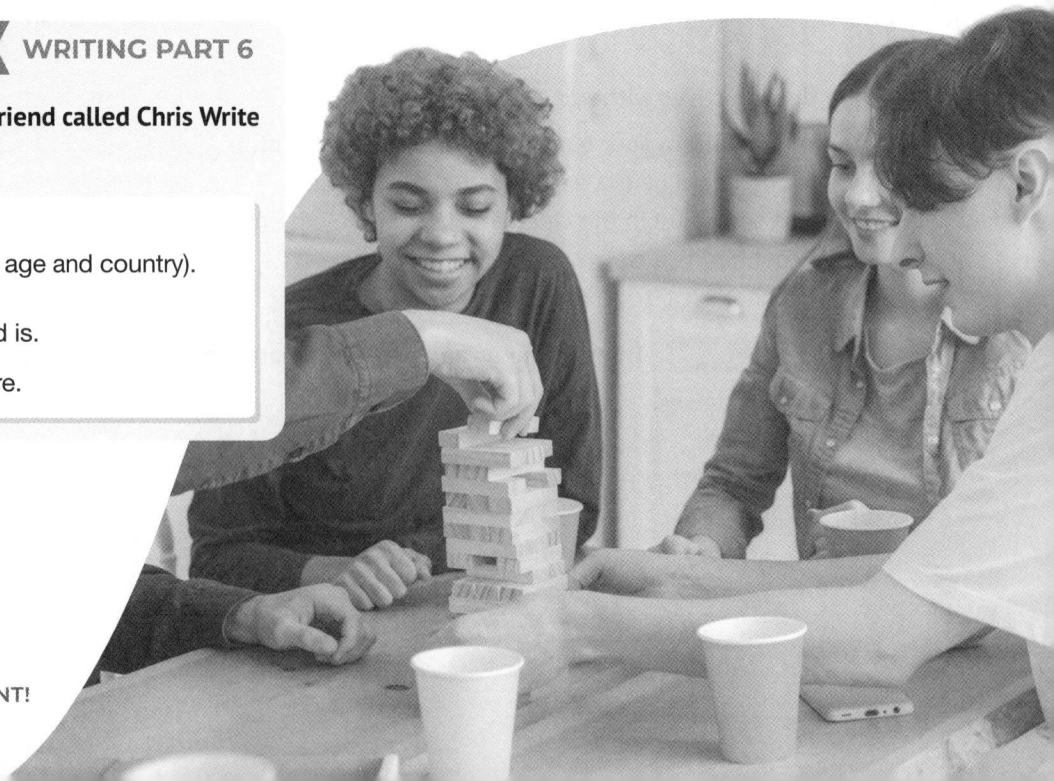

GRAMMAR

1 Choose the correct words to complete the questions.

1 *What / Where / How* are you from? I'm from Mumbai in India.
2 *Why / What / How* old are you? I'm 11.
3 *Who / Why / What* 's your name? My name's Gina.
4 *What / Where / Why* do you like films? Because they're fun.
5 *Who / What / How* is your favourite singer? Shawn Mendes.

2 Complete the text with the words in the box.

> his   its   my   our   their   your

Hi! ¹ _____ name's Maia and I live in New Zealand. My best friend is my brother. ² _____ name is Keanu. We love hiking at the weekend with ³ _____ mum and dad! ⁴ _____ names are Alice and Mateo. The dog likes hiking too! ⁵ _____ name is Kuri. What are ⁶ _____ favourite things?

3 Complete the conversations with the correct form of *be*.

1 A: _____ you at home?
   B: No, I _____. I _____ in class.
2 A: How old _____ your brother?
   B: He _____ 16.
3 A: _____ your friends at the party?
   B: No, they _____. They _____ at the cinema.
4 A: _____ we all here?
   B: No, Danny _____ here.
5 A: _____ your favourite colour green?
   B: No, it _____. My favourite colours _____ pink and purple.

VOCABULARY

1 Write these words in the correct place.

> band   bike   board game   camera
> cinema   comic book   cycling   guitar
> hiking   online gaming   party

Music: _____band_____, _____
Film: _____
Sport: _____, _____, _____
Games _____, _____
Other: _____, _____, _____

2 Choose the correct words to complete the sentences.

1 More than eight million people live in New York. It's a *big / small* city.
2 I really like online gaming because it's *fun / important*.
3 That game is €3. I want it! It's very *cheap / expensive*.
4 My brother is great at cycling. He's very *slow / fast*.
5 I love my town. It's 200 years old and it's *new / beautiful*.

SELF-ASSESSMENT!

How confident do you feel about:

- using question words? ☹ 😐 😐 🙂
- using possessive adjectives? ☹ 😐 😐 🙂
- using the present simple of *be*? ☹ 😐 😐 🙂
- talking about your favourite things and activities? ☹ 😐 😐 🙂
- using the numbers 0–20? ☹ 😐 😐 🙂
- describing things? ☹ 😐 😐 🙂

I WANT TO FIND OUT MORE ABOUT THE PEOPLE IN MY CLASS.

1 THINK

My partner is:

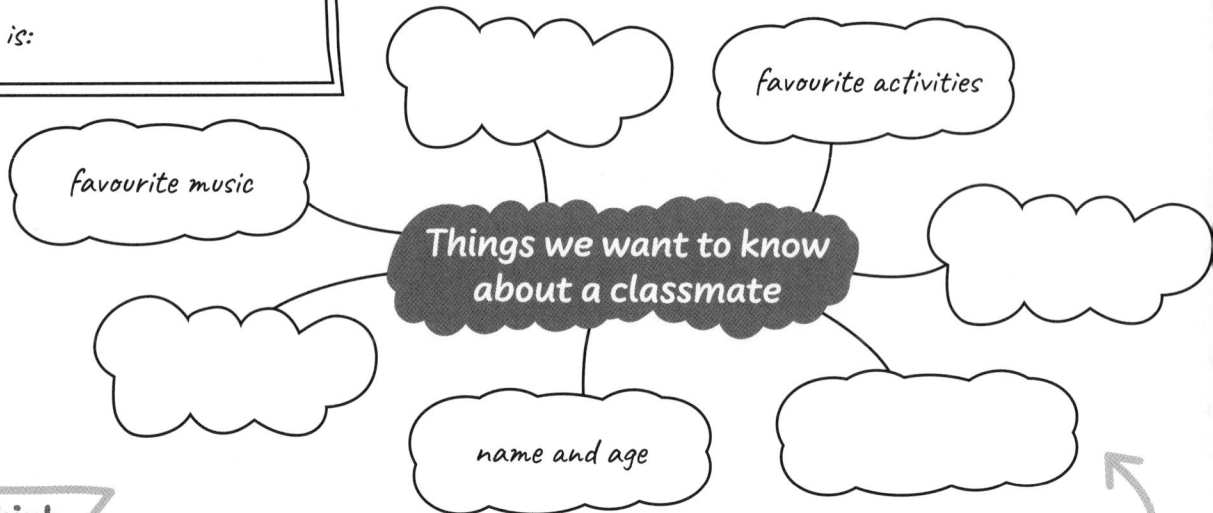

favourite music

favourite activities

Things we want to know about a classmate

name and age

Tip for Think

Think about people, animals and places in your classmate's life.

What else can you ask about? Complete the spidergram with your ideas.

2 PREPARE

My group is:

Tip for Prepare

Look at your Student's Book for examples of questions.

Our questions:

_____

_____

_____

_____

_____

We want to ask _____
(How many?) questions.
We want to ask about:

_____

_____

③ DEVELOP

My classmate to interview is: _____

My classmate's answers:

_____
_____
_____
_____
_____

Write your classmate's answers here.

Tip for Develop

You don't need to write the full answers. Make notes.

④ PRESENT

| Name and age | Other things | Favourite things and activities |

Put your notes in order for your presentation.

Tip for Present

Look at your classmates and your teacher when you present.

Draw a face to show how you feel.

SELF-EVALUATION

I can ...

- think of questions to find out about a classmate. ◯
- work with a group to select and organise our questions for an interview. ◯
- interview a classmate and write their answers. ◯
- present my information to the class. ◯

UNIT 2 MY PEOPLE

VOCABULARY

FAMILY MEMBERS

1 Find 11 family words in the wordsearch.

A	U	N	C	L	E	D	G
G	R	A	N	D	P	A	R
S	M	U	M	A	D	U	A
O	B	N	S	D	E	G	N
N	N	T	U	R	M	H	D
C	O	U	S	I	N	T	M
S	I	S	T	E	R	E	A
B	R	O	T	H	E	R	P

2 Look at the family tree and answer the questions.

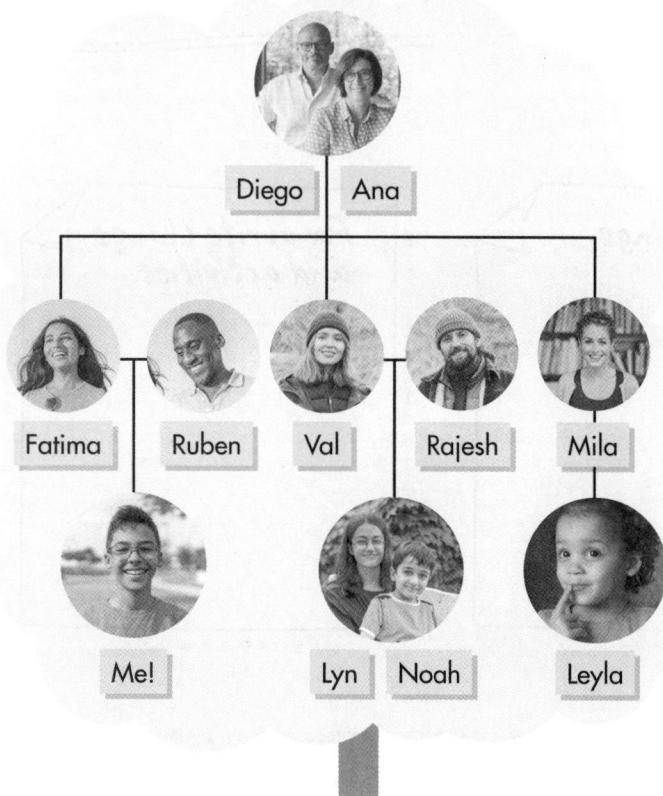

Diego   Ana

Fatima   Ruben   Val   Rajesh   Mila

Me!   Lyn   Noah   Leyla

1 Who are my mum and dad? _____ and _____

2 Who are my grandma and grandpa? _____ and _____

3 Who is my uncle? _____

4 Who is Noah's sister? _____

5 Who is Lyn's brother? _____

6 Who are my cousins? _____, _____ and _____

7 Who are Val's son and daughter? _____ and _____

3 Look at the family tree again and complete the sentences with the words in the box.

> aunts brothers cousins dad daughter
> grandma grandpa mum sisters son uncle

1 Hi! This is my family tree. Ruben is my _____ and Fatima is my _____.

2 Fatima, Val and Mila are _____. Val and Mila are my _____.

3 Rajesh is my _____ and he's married to Val. Noah is their _____ and Lyn is their _____.

4 Noah and Lyn are great fun. They're my _____.

5 My little cousin Leyla is cool! She hasn't got any _____ or sisters. She's an only child like me.

6 Ana is our _____ and Diego is our _____. We all love cycling with them!

4 Use the tree to show some people in your family. Write their names and who they are (dad, grandma, etc.). Draw pictures of them if you want.

Me

AN ARTICLE

1 Look at the photo and read the title of the article. Why do you think this family is famous?

2 Read the article and check your ideas in Exercise 1.

WHY ARE THE *Kanneh-Masons* FAMOUS?

The Kanneh-Masons are a cool family. The mum's name is Dr Kadiatu Kanneh and she's from Sierra Leone in West Africa. The dad's name is Stuart Mason. He's from London, England, but his parents are from Antigua in the Caribbean.

Kadiatu and Stuart have seven children – and they are all famous <u>musicians</u>! They play <u>concerts</u> around the world. Their music is on the radio too.

That's Isata, one of the daughters, in this photo. She plays the <u>piano</u>. Her four sisters also play the piano. And that's Sheku Kanneh-Mason, one of Isata's brothers. Sheku plays the <u>cello</u> and he's very famous in the UK.

The last child in this family is Mariatu. She's famous, too – she plays the piano and the cello. She also goes to school because she's a young teen.

3 Read the article again. Choose the correct words to complete the sentences.

1 Kadiatu Kanneh is from *Sierra Leone / England*.
2 There are *four / seven* children in the family.
3 The *children / parents and children* are musicians.
4 Isata plays the *piano / cello*.
5 Sheku is Isata's *sister / brother*.
6 Mariatu is a *teacher / student*.

4 Look at the <u>underlined</u> words in the text and look at the photo. How do you say these words in your language?

5 🎯 Critical Thinking Find out about a famous family in your country. Why are they famous?

6 Read the text in the exam task quickly. How many people are in the Torres family? _____

EXAM TIP

Remember to write <u>one</u> word only in each gap in the task.

☑ EXAM TRAINING READING PART 5

7 For each question, write the correct answer. Write ONE word for each gap in the task.

Yes Day

Yes Day is a film about ⁰ ___an___ American family. Allison is married to Carlos Torres. Katie, Nando and Ellen ¹ _____ their children . Katie is 14 and ² _____ wants to see her favourite band. Do her parents say 'yes'?

I like this film because ³ _____ favourite actor, Jenna Ortega, is in it.

GRAMMAR

THIS, THAT, THESE, THOSE

1 **Match the sentences to the photos.**

1 **This** is my favourite book.
2 **Those** aren't her shoes!
3 **These** are my cousins.
4 **That**'s a cool guitar.

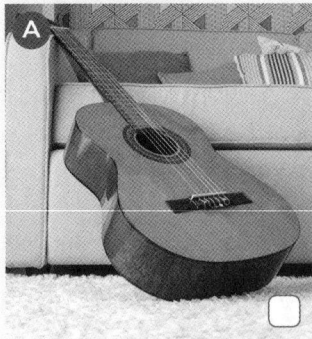

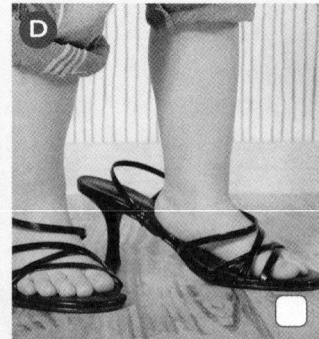

2 **Choose the correct words to complete the sentences.**

1 Who's *that / those* girl in the photo? Is she your cousin?
2 Are *this / these* your comic books? I want to read one.
3 *This / These* isn't my bag. My bag is blue.
4 *These / Those* guitars in the shop in town aren't expensive.
5 *This / That* is a beautiful city! I love it here.
6 Look at *these / those* pictures on my phone. I think they're cool.

POSSESSIVE 'S

3 **Complete the words with 's or s'.**

Here's a cool photo of our ¹group_____ presentation. Our ²teacher_____ name is Mr Jones and he's very nice. I'm at the front with my friends. The other ³boy_____ names are Mel and Ben. ⁴Mel_____ cousins are in our class too, but his ⁵cousin_____ desks are at the back.

4 **Write the sentences with the possessive 's or s'.**

My sister / name / is / Carla
My sister's name is Carla.

1 Max / camera / is / new.
_____

2 My cousins / band / is called / Green Ball
_____

3 Our town / cinemas / are / cheap
_____

4 The teacher / email / is / important
_____

5 My friends / names / are / Finn and Aisha
_____

6 Those girls / bikes / are / fast
_____

HAVE(N'T) GOT

5 **Put the words in the correct order.**

1 a new board game / I / got / 've / .
_____

2 got / any paper / We / got / haven't / .
_____

3 My dad / any cousins / got / hasn't / .
_____

4 've / You / a beautiful house / got / .
_____

5 a bike / got / Has / your uncle / ?
_____

6 have / got / What / in their garden / your grandma and grandpa / ?
_____

6 Complete the conversation with the correct form of *have got*.

Ethan: ¹ _____ you _____ a big family?

Lia: Yes, I ² _____, but I ³ _____ any brothers. I ⁴ _____ lots of cousins, because my mum ⁵ _____ four brothers and sisters. ⁶ _____ your mum _____ any brothers and sisters?

Ethan: No, she ⁷ _____. Our family is small, but we ⁸ _____ a cat and a dog.

Lia: Oh, that's nice!

7 ⟫⟫ **STRETCH!** Find one mistake in each sentence and correct it.

1 My aunt name is Julia.

   _____

2 You have got a little brother?

   _____

3 My friends bags are in the classroom.

   _____

4 My sister hasn't a favourite singer.

   _____

5 Who's this girl in your grandma's garden?

   _____

6 Come and look. Those are my new books.

   _____

VOCABULARY

DESCRIBING PEOPLE

1 Read the descriptions and match them to five people in the photo. There is one extra person.

Meet my friends!

a Kelly's got <u>long</u>, <u>blonde</u> hair and she's <u>young</u>.

   _____

b Adam is <u>tall</u>. He's got <u>short</u>, <u>curly</u> hair and glasses.

   _____

c Di's <u>short</u> and she's got <u>straight</u>, <u>dark</u> hair.

   _____

d Liam is on the left. His hair is <u>short</u> and <u>dark</u>.

   _____

e Matt's my cousin. His hair is <u>short</u> and <u>blonde</u>. He isn't <u>old</u>.

   _____

2 Complete the lists with the <u>underlined</u> words in Exercise 1. One of the words goes in two lists.

Hair

_____   _____

_____   _____

_____   _____

Height

_____   _____

Age

_____   _____

3 Write a description for the extra person in the photo. Use at least three of the adjectives in Exercise 2.

_____

_____

WRITING

AN EMAIL

1 Read Luke's email to his new online friend, Ellie. Then answer the questions.

< Inbox   ∧ ∨

From: Luke
To: Ellie

Subject: An important person

Hi Ellie

I want to tell you about my cousin. Her name is Jody and she's great fun! She's tall and she's got short, curly hair. She's 13 and she's got a little brother, Ned. He's two and he's got long, blonde hair.

Jody's dad is my mum's brother. He's a singer in a band but the band isn't famous.

Write back soon about an important person in your life.

Bye for now,

Luke

---

1 Who is the important person?

2 What does she look like?

3 Has she got any brothers or sisters?

4 What's the boy's hair like?

5 Who's in a band?

2 Choose an important person in your life. Use one of the ideas below or your own idea. Then make notes in the table.

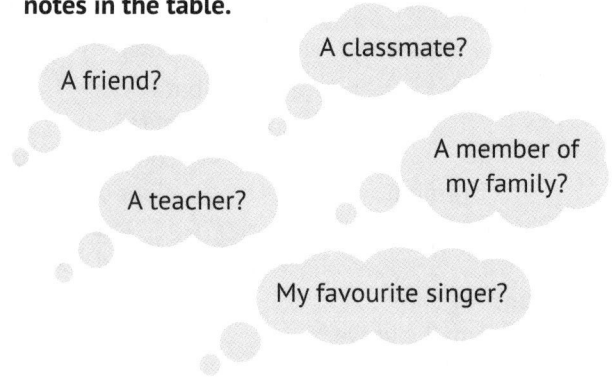

A friend?

A classmate?

A teacher?

A member of my family?

My favourite singer?

Who?	
Age	
Height	
Hair	
Other information	

3 Write an email to an English friend about your important person. Use your notes from Exercise 2.

LISTENING

SHORT DIALOGUES

EXAM TIP

Before you listen, look at each picture. How are they different?

1 Look at the pictures in the exam task. How are they different?

☑ EXAM TRAINING ‹ LISTENING PART 1

2 ◁)) 2.01 For each question, choose the correct answer.

1 Which boy is John's friend?

2 Who is in the boy's photo?

UNIT 2 REVIEW

GRAMMAR

1 Complete the sentences with *this*, *that*, *these* or *those*.

1 Look over there! _____ is my cousin Kerry.

2 _____ homework is difficult. Can you help me?

3 Are _____ your sisters' friends? It's difficult to see them from here.

4 What's _____? Is it a dog in your garden?

5 Look at _____ pictures in this book. They're beautiful.

6 _____ boys over there are in my class.

2 Rewrite the sentences with the apostrophe (') in the correct place.

1 Our teachers phone is white.

_____

2 My grandmas bike is really fast.

_____

3 Charlies parents house is old and beautiful.

_____

4 Lilys parties are always great fun.

_____

5 My cousins names are Marek and Eva.

_____

3 Complete the email with the correct form of *have got*.

Inbox   2 Messages   ∧ ∨

Hi Zoe

I want to tell you about my family.
I ¹ _____ a sister but I ² _____ any brothers. My sister's name is Luisa and she ³ _____ short, curly hair. We love animals but we ⁴ _____ a pet. My aunt ⁵ _____ a cat. His name is Miki.
⁶ _____ you _____ a big family?

Lee

VOCABULARY

1 Use these words to answer the questions.

aunt   brother   cousin
grandma   grandpa   uncle

1 Who is your mum's son?   my _____
2 Who is your dad's mum?   my _____
3 Who is your father's sister? my _____
4 Who is your cousin's dad?   my _____
5 Who is your cousin's brother?   my _____
6 Who is your mum's dad?   my _____

2 Complete the adjectives to describe people.

HOME   BLOG   CONTACT   🔍

My favourite ★ ★ ★ ★ ★
family members

My sister is my best friend, but she doesn't look like me. I'm tall but she's
¹ sh_____. I've got curly hair, but she's got
² l_____, ³ str_____ hair. My hair is dark, but her hair is ⁴ blo_____. I've also got a little brother. He's great. He's only two, so he's very yo_____.

ASKING QUESTIONS

1 ASKING FOR MORE INFORMATION

Think of things you want to know about members of your partner's family.

My partner is:

Add your own ideas.

Family members:

dad   sister

name

age

what they look like

favourite things

pets

Write all the words you know.

What are some questions you can ask?

How old ...?   Is he ...?   Has she got ...?   Are they ...?   Have you got ...?

Is he ...?   What's your uncle's name?   How many ...?   Who's ...?

Has your mum got any brothers?   What's ...?

_____

_____

_____

2 ASKING FOR CLARIFICATION

Complete the sentences with these words.

| repeat right this those understand |

When something isn't clear, I can say:

Sorry, I don't ¹_____.

I can also ask questions:

Is that ²_____?

Are ³_____ your cousins?

Can you ⁴_____ that?

Is ⁵_____ your aunt?

Other useful expressions:

Can you speak more clearly, please?

_____

> You can draw your partner's family tree here.

> Think of another expression in your language.
>
> Use a dictionary for help and then check with your teacher.

| Have you got some photos you can share with your partner? |

CHECKLIST

	Me	My partner
Asking for clarification: Is that right?		
Asking for information: How many ... have you got?		

UNIT 3 LET'S EAT!

VOCABULARY

FOOD, DRINK AND CONTAINERS

1 Write the food words under the photos.

> fruit juice milkshake noodles
> salad sandwich soup vegetables

2 Complete the diagram with five words from Exercise 1. There are two extra words. What are they and what is their container?

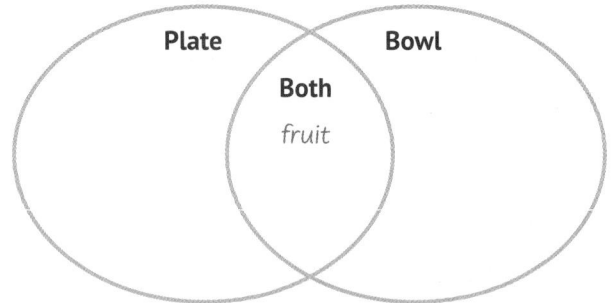

Plate

Bowl

Both

fruit

3 Choose the correct words to complete the post.

Q A What's your favourite **FOOD** or **DRINK?**

This milkshake is my favourite drink. I've got milk, fresh [1] *noodles / fruit* and ice cream in my [2] *glass / plate*. 😊

[3] *Juice / Salad* is great food for a hot day. I put lettuce and other [4] *sandwiches / vegetables* in a bowl. Yum!

I've got a [5] *bowl / bottle* of cold water in my bag. That's my favourite drink.

4 🛡 **Creative Thinking** Create an unusual sandwich. Use food words on this page or think of other food words. Draw a picture and label it.

READING

SHORT TEXTS

1 Look at the photos of food (A–C). Then read the title of the text in the exam task. What do you think *breakfast* is?

   a the first meal of the day

   b the meal you have at night

2 Read both texts in the exam task. Then look again at photos A–C and complete the sentences.

   1 Lucas's breakfast is in photo _____.

   2 Aki's breakfast is in photo _____.

✓ EXAM TRAINING   READING PART 2

3 For each question, choose the correct answer.

		Lucas	Aki
1	Who lives in a big place?	A	B
2	Who has fruit for breakfast?	A	B
3	Who eats with their grandparents every day?	A	B
4	Who has got a sister?	A	B

WHAT'S FOR BREAKFAST?

LUCAS

I live in a small town in Chile with my parents. In the morning, I have bread and fruit and a glass of juice for breakfast. Then I walk to school. At the weekend, I have breakfast with my grandparents. They live in Santiago. That's a big city in Chile. I love the milkshakes at the café near their house.

AKI

I live with my grandparents and my aunt in Osaka in Japan. My city is big, and the food here is great. In our home, breakfast is a big meal. We all eat together. We have vegetables, rice and a bowl of soup. In the evening, we have noodles or soup, and also fruit.

4 <u>Underline</u> the food and drink words in the texts. How do you say the new words in your language?

5 What's for breakfast in your home? Draw a picture and label it.

GRAMMAR

THERE IS / ARE, THERE ISN'T / AREN'T

1 Complete the table with the words in the box.

> ~~bottle~~ bowl ~~bread~~ egg flour fruit glass juice plate sandwich soup strawberry sugar water

Countable	Uncountable
bottle	bread

2 Choose the correct words to complete the sentences.

1 There's *a / some / any* pen on the table.
2 There isn't *a / some / any* fruit in the bowl.
3 There isn't *a / some / any* café near my house.
4 There aren't *a / some / any* new students in my class.
5 There are *a / some / any* books on the desk.
6 There are *a / some / any* vegetables in the garden.

3 Look at the photos. Complete the sentences with *is, are, isn't* or *aren't* and *a, some* or *any*.

1 There _____ _____ juice in the bottle.

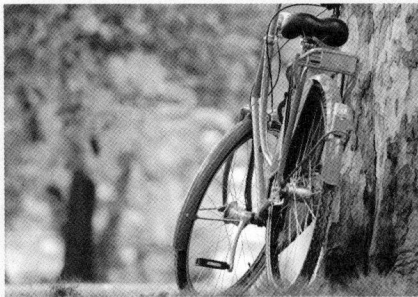

2 There _____ _____ bike here.

3 There _____ _____ bread on the table.

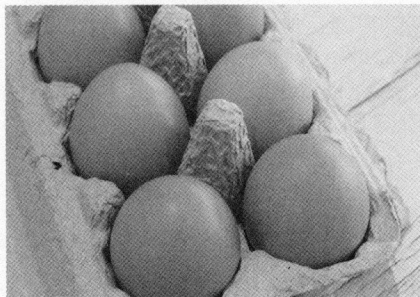

4 There _____ _____ eggs in that box.

5 There _____ _____ people in the cinema.

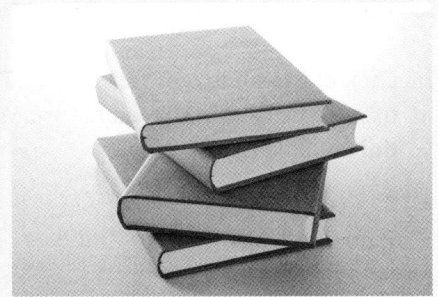

6 There _____ _____ books in this picture.

IS THERE / ARE THERE QUESTIONS, *MUCH, MANY, A LOT (OF)*

4 Complete the questions with *Is there* or *Are there*?

1 _____ any juice in that glass?
2 _____ an apple in the fruit bowl?
3 _____ any new films on TV?
4 _____ any board games in that box?
5 _____ a girl with long hair in your class?
6 _____ any juice for breakfast?

5 Choose the correct words to complete the quiz. Then choose the correct answers.

QUESTION TIME!

1 How ¹ *many / much* different kinds of pizza are there?

  A There aren't ² *many / much* different kinds.

  B There are ³ *a lot of / much* different kinds.

2 How ⁴ *many / much* water is there in our body?

  A There isn't ⁵ *many / much* water.

  B There's ⁶ *a lot of / much* water.

3 How ⁷ *many / much* metres are there in one kilometre?

  A There aren't ⁸ *many / much* metres.

  B There are 1,000 metres.

6 Complete the questions with *How much* or *How many* and the correct form of *be*.

1 _____ blue pens _____ there in your pencil case?

2 _____ juice _____ there in your kitchen?

3 _____ students _____ there in your class?

4 _____ chocolate _____ there in your bag?

5 _____ fruit _____ there in your kitchen?

6 _____ parks _____ there in your town?

7 ⟫⟫ **STRETCH!** Write your answers to the questions in Exercise 6.

1 _____
2 _____
3 _____
4 _____
5 _____
6 _____

VOCABULARY

NUMBERS 20–100

1 Write the numbers in words.

20

1 _____

30

2 _____

40

3 _____

50

4 _____

60

5 _____

70

6 _____

80

7 _____

90

8 _____

100

9 _____

2 Look at the photos and write the numbers in words.

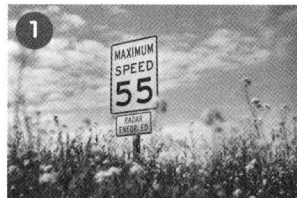

1
fifty-five

2
_____

3
_____

4
_____

5
_____

6
_____ and _____

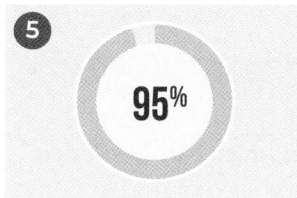

3 Find three numbers (20–100) at home, in your school or outside. Draw pictures or take photos of them and write the numbers in words.

WRITING

A MESSAGE

1 Look at the photos and read Ania's message. Tick (✓) what she wants for lunch.

1

2

3

Dad
Online

A Hi Dad!

B I need lunch for my school trip tomorrow. I want to make some sandwiches, but there isn't much bread. There aren't many tomatoes and there isn't any cheese.

C There isn't much fruit in the bowl. We haven't got any bananas or apples. I've got my water bottle but is there any juice?

D Can you get what I need at the shops, please?

E Thanks a lot!

Ania

2 Read the message again. In which part (A–E) does Ania …

1 say thank you? _____

2 talk about something to drink? _____

3 say hello? _____

4 say why she needs some food? _____

5 ask her dad to go shopping? _____

3 Choose one of these situations or your own idea. Write a message to a person in your family. Ask them to get some food.

- You want to make breakfast for your grandma.
- You want to have a meal in the park with some friends.
- You want to take some food to a football match.

LISTENING

A CONVERSATION

1 What's your favourite restaurant? What's your favourite thing to eat or drink at the restaurant?

2 🔊 3.01 Listen to Amina talking to Hassan about her favourite restaurant. What's the name of the restaurant?

EXAM TIP

You will hear information about all the answers (A, B and C). Listen carefully for the correct answer.

☑ EXAM TRAINING · LISTENING PART 3

3 🔊 3.02 For each question, choose the correct answer.

> You will hear Amina talking to Hassan about her favourite restaurant.
>
> **1** Amina's favourite restaurant is near the …
>   A park.
>   B school.
>   C cinema.
> **2** What's Amina favourite drink at the restaurant?
>   A a milkshake
>   B water
>   C juice

4 🎖 Critical Thinking Look at your answers in Exercise 1 again. Is your favourite restaurant a good place for a birthday meal? Why? / Why not?

GRAMMAR

1 Write *C* (countable) or *U* (uncountable).

1 cheese ___ 4 candle ___
2 water ___ 5 sugar ___
3 egg ___ 6 grapes ___

2 Complete the sentences with the words in the box.

> a an any are is some

1 There's _____ beautiful park in our town.
2 There's _____ apple in the bowl.
3 There _____ some pencils on my desk.
4 There's _____ milk in my glass.
5 There aren't _____ English books in this box.
6 There _____ some food on the table.

3 Choose the correct words to complete the sentences.

Jake: It's Yuri's birthday and I want to make a cake. ¹ *Is / Are* there any chocolate?

Gita: There isn't ² *much / many* chocolate but there are ³ *much / a lot of* eggs.

Jake: How ⁴ *much / many* flour is there?

Gita: There isn't ⁵ *any / some* flour.

Jake: And how ⁶ *much / many* candles are there?

Gita: We've got 14 candles. And Yuri's 13, right?

Jake: That's right! Perfect.

VOCABULARY

1 Complete the table with the words in the box.

> bottle bowl fruit glass juice
> milkshake noodles plate salad
> sandwich soup vegetables

Food	Drink	Container

2 Write the numbers in words.

1 58 _____
2 99 _____
3 24 _____
4 46 _____
5 35 _____
6 72 _____
7 81 _____
8 37 _____
9 60 _____
10 93 _____

SELF-ASSESSMENT!

How confident do you feel about:

- using countable and uncountable nouns? ☹ ☺ 😐 ☺
- using *there is / isn't* and *there are / aren't*? ☹ ☺ 😐 ☺
- using *a*, *some* and *any*? ☹ ☺ 😐 ☺
- using *much*, *many* and *a lot (of)*? ☹ ☺ 😐 ☺
- talking about food, drink and containers? ☹ ☺ 😐 ☺
- saying and writing the numbers 20–100? ☹ ☺ 😐 ☺

I WANT TO KNOW MORE ABOUT THE FOOD I EAT.

1 THINK

My group is:

Food we love to eat:

Tips for Think

Write down a lot of different kinds of food. Then choose one food you all like for Stage 2.

Is the food good for us? If yes, tick (√) it.

2 PREPARE

Is it cheap or expensive?

Do you need to cook it?

Our food is

Other information:

Where is it from (a tree? an animal? ...)

What information do you know? What do you need to find out?

Tips for Prepare

Listen to each other and ask questions. To find more information, look online or in a book.

③ DEVELOP

Plan your poster in your group.

What's the title?

What's in the picture?

What information is in the sentences?
- •
- •
- •
- •

Write your notes.
Then choose one person
to draw the picture.
The others write
the sentences.

Title

Choose the best place
for your picture and
the best places for
your sentences.

Tips for Develop

Write your sentences
in your notebook first.
Then check them
together before
you write them
on the poster.

④ PRESENT

Our presenter is:

Our group's practice

😊 😐

Write down the good and not so
good things about the practice.
The tell the presenter.
Remember to be kind!

SELF-EVALUATION

I can ...
- discuss different types of food. ◯
- share information about one type of food and do some research to find out more. ◯
- plan a poster with my group to present the food. ◯
- give helpful feedback to my group's presenter. ◯

Tips for Present

Listen to the other groups'
presentations. Think of one good
thing you can tell the presenter.
You can also ask questions.

JUICE

UNIT 4 GAMES, GAMES, GAMES!

VOCABULARY

SPORTS AND GAMES VERBS

1 Find 12 verbs for sports and games in the word snake.

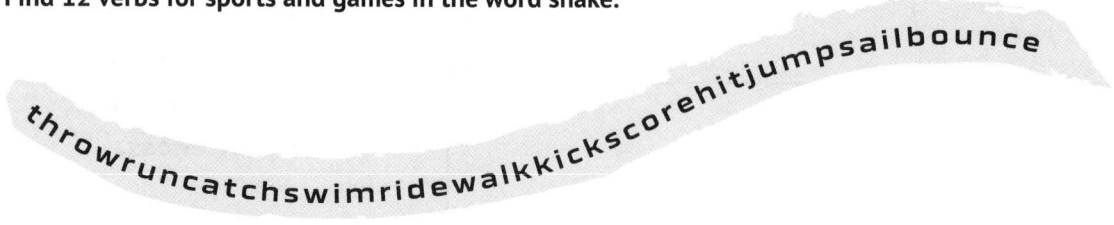

throwruncatchswimridewalkkickscorehitjumpsailbounce

2 Complete the crossword using the clues and verbs from Exercise 1.

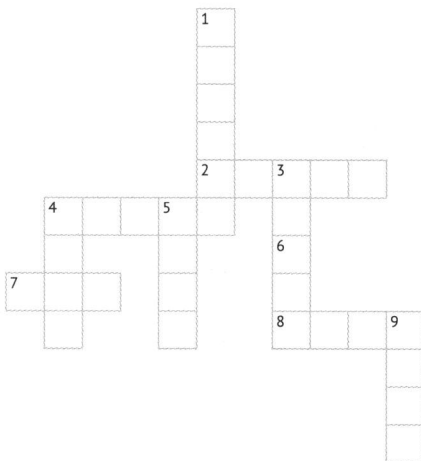

Across ➜

2 4 6 7 8

Down ↓

1 3 4 5 9

3 Complete the diagram with the words in the box.

> bounce catch jump kick
> run sail swim throw walk

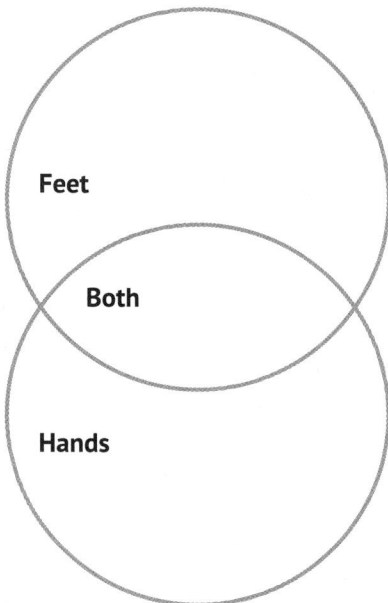

Feet

Both

Hands

4 Complete the descriptions with the words in the box.

> bounce catch jump kick ride run sail score swim walk

HOME **FORUM** VIDEOS Search …

WHAT'S YOUR FAVOURITE SPORT?

This week we ask our readers about their favourite sport.

In summer, my family ¹ _____ in our boat. I also ² _____ in the water and ³ _____ in the sea.

Marcus, 13

I don't like water sports. I have fun when I ⁴ _____ my bike or ⁵ _____ in the mountains with my family.

Tom, 12

My favourite sport is basketball. It's fun to ⁶ _____ fast and ⁷ _____ the ball on the floor. My friend throws the ball and I always ⁸ _____ it.

Aisha, 14

I don't like basketball. I prefer football because you can ⁹ _____ the ball and ¹⁰ _____ a goal.

Saida, 11

READING

REAL-WORLD TEXTS

1 Match the photos (A–D) to the text types (1–4).

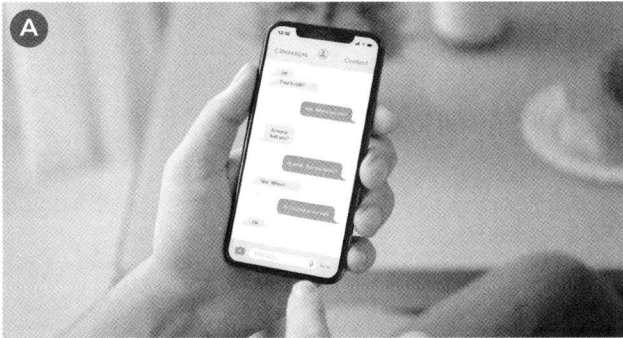

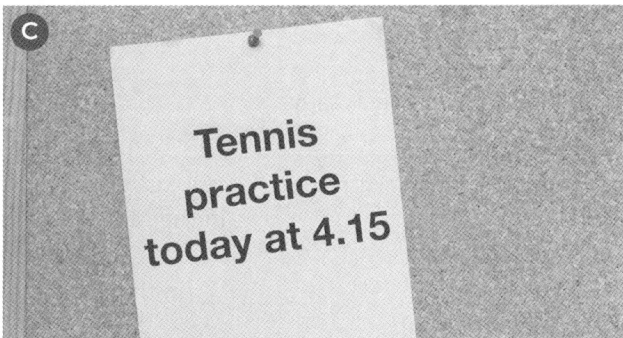

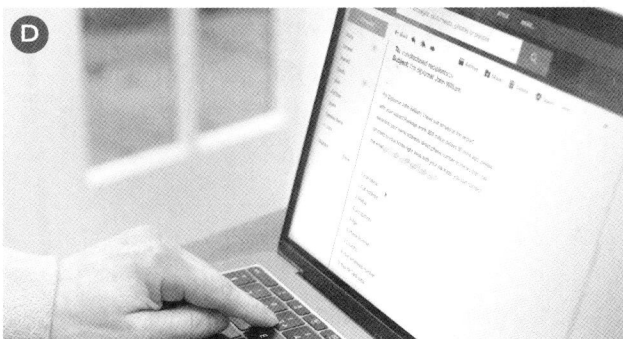

NO PARKING
GATE IN USE
24 HOURS

Tennis practice today at 4.15

1	a sign _____	3	an email _____
2	a message _____	4	a notice _____

2 Look quickly at the exam task. What kinds of texts can you see?

1 _____ 3 _____

2 _____

EXAM TIP

All three options (A–C) are about the text, but only <u>one</u> is correct.

---

3 For each question, choose the correct answer.

1

HALE SPORTS CENTRE

The pool is closed today from 1 pm for a school party.

A The sports centre is open in the morning.
B The pool is only for students.
C The sports centre is always closed in the afternoon.

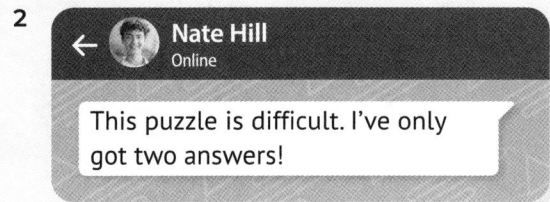

2

← **Nate Hill** Online

This puzzle is difficult. I've only got two answers!

A Nate loves doing this puzzle.
B Nate can answer some questions.
C Nate has got all the answers.

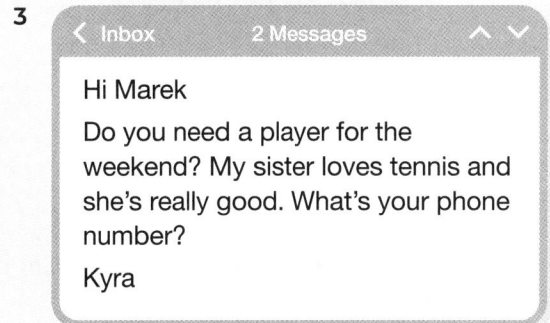

3

‹ Inbox   2 Messages   ∧ ∨

Hi Marek

Do you need a player for the weekend? My sister loves tennis and she's really good. What's your phone number?

Kyra

A Kyra loves all kinds of sports.
B Kyra wants Marek's number.
C Kyra plays tennis very well.

4 🞧 **Creative Thinking** Choose one of these situations or your own idea. Write a short message.

- It's a friend's birthday.
- You want to play tennis at the weekend.
- You can't do your homework.

GRAMMAR

CAN FOR ABILITY

1 Complete the sentences with *can* or *can't*.

1 I _____ ride   2 He _____
   a horse.   kick a ball.

3 She _____   4 They _____
   walk.   draw well.

5 It _____
   jump.

2 Look at the table. Write sentences with *can* or *can't*.

	Ruth	Zahra	Luis
⛵	✓	✗	✗
🍳	✗	✓	✓
⚽	✓	✓	✗

1 Ruth / sail
   _____

2 Luis / score a goal
   _____

3 Zahra and Luis / cook
   _____

4 Zahra and Luis / sail
   _____

5 Ruth / cook
   _____

6 Ruth and Zahra / score a goal
   _____

3 Complete these conversations with the correct form of *can* and the verb in brackets.

1 A: _____ you _____ (run) fast?
   B: Yes, I _____.

2 A: _____ your cousin _____
      (swim)?
   B: No, she _____.

3 A: _____ your dad _____ (play)
      the guitar?
   B: Yes, he _____.

4 A: _____ your friends _____
      (cook)?
   B: Yes, they _____.

5 A: _____ you and your sister
      _____ (ride) a scooter?
   B: No, we _____.

LIKE, LOVE, DON'T LIKE, ETC. + -ING FORMS

4 Complete the sentences with the correct form of the verbs.

1 I _____ to the cinema.
   (love / go)

2 We _____ our homework.
   (not mind / do)

3 My brothers _____ comic
   books. (not like / read)

4 My friends _____ in a band.
   (like / play)

5 You _____ in the rain.
   (hate / walk)

6 My dog _____ in the sea.
   (love / swim).

5 Look at the emojis and write the sentences.

1 My friends / 🙂 kick / a ball in the park.
   _____

2 I / 🙁 watch / films on TV.
   _____

3 We / 😣 swim / in cold water.
   _____

4 My mum / 😐 walk / to work.
   _____

5 You / 😍 play / board games.
   _____

6 Complete the post with the words in the box.

doing   don't   don't   hate   like   mind

HOME   BLOGS   CONTACT

I love ¹ _____ a lot of different activities. I'm good at most sports. I ² _____ playing tennis and I'm good at it. My sisters ³ _____ like running but I don't ⁴ _____ it. The only sport I ⁵ _____ is sailing! That's because I can't swim very well.

7 **⟫ STRETCH!** Read the questions and write answers that are true for you.

1   Can you make soup?

_____

2   Can you play a musical instrument?

_____

3   What do you like doing after school?

_____

4   What do you like doing at the weekend?

_____

5   What do your friends like doing at the weekend?

_____

VOCABULARY

SPORTS AND GAMES NOUNS

1 Complete the sports and games words with *a, e, i, o* and *u*.

1   p__zzl__
2   c__mp__t__t____n
3   sp__rts c__ntr__
4   ch__ss
5   pl__y__r
6   sw__mm__ng p_____l
7   pr__z__
8   r__ll__r sk__t__s

2 Choose the correct words to complete the sentences.

1   We can go fast on roller *skates / sports*.
2   The football World Cup is a big *player / competition*.
3   People can play tennis at the sports *pool / centre*.
4   I can't find the answer to this *puzzle / chess*!
5   You're the winner! You get a *plate / prize*!

3 Complete the blog post with the correct form of the words in Exercise 1.

HOME ▶   BLOG ▶   LOG IN ▶

What do I like doing after school?

I swim in the ¹ _____ in the ² _____ near the cinema after school. I usually go there on my ³ _____. At the weekend, there are ⁴ _____ and I sometimes win a ⁵ _____. I also like playing ⁶ _____ with my uncle. He's a very good ⁷ _____. We sometimes do ⁸ _____ together, too. They're difficult, but they're fun.

What about you? What do you like doing after school?

WRITING

A BLOG POST

1 Read Megan's blog post. Then correct the information in the sentences.

HOME ﹀   BLOGS ﹀   CONTACT ﹀

MY FRIENDS AND I: SIMILAR BUT DIFFERENT!

I've got a lot of good friends, and we have a lot of fun together. Some of them love going to the swimming pool, but I don't like doing that. I can't swim very well. One of my friends, Annie, likes playing chess. She's the best player in our school. I love playing with her because she teaches me new things. We all love going to the park to play football. What about you and your friends? Are you very similar? How are you different?

1 Megan hasn't got many friends.

_____

2 Megan is good at swimming.

_____

3 Annie is a teacher at Megan's school.

_____

4 Megan doesn't like playing chess.

_____

5 Megan and her friends hate going to the park.

_____

2 In which order does Megan do these things?

a ☐ She talks about some of her friends.
b ☐ She asks a question.
c ☐ She says how many friends she's got.
d ☐ She talks about all of her friends.
e ☐ She talks about one of her friends.

3 Write a blog post about you and your friends. How are you similar? How are you different?

LISTENING

A CONVERSATION

1 Look at the activities (A–E) in the exam task and match them to the photos.

EXAM TIP

When you hear an answer, c̶r̶o̶s̶s̶ ̶o̶u̶t̶ the person and the activity.

☑ EXAM TRAINING   LISTENING PART 5

2 ◁)) **4.01 For each question, choose the correct answer.**
You will hear Simon talking to his friend Mara about his family. What is each person good at?

People		Activities
0 s̶i̶s̶t̶e̶r̶	D	A guitar
1 brother	☐	B chess
2 aunt	☐	C swimming
		D t̶e̶n̶n̶i̶s̶
		E cycling

3 🎓 Critical Thinking **Think of a new activity that you want to do. How can you learn to do this activity? Who can help you?**

GRAMMAR

1 Write sentences with *can* or *can't*.

1 I / dance (✗)

_____

2 My mum / run very fast (✓)

_____

3 He / play the guitar well (✓)

_____

4 Our team / score goals today (✗)

_____

5 I / kick a ball (✓)

_____

6 My friends / play chess (✗)

_____

2 Put the words in the correct order.

1 love / We / sport on TV / watching / .

_____

2 like / My brothers / comic books / reading / don't / .

_____

3 sandwiches for dinner / don't / I / having / mind / .

_____

4 hiking / like / in the mountains / My friends / .

_____

5 to school / hate / You / walking / .

_____

6 pizza / My grandpa / loves / for everyone / making / .

_____

3 Complete the conversation with the words in the box.

can   can't   don't   mind   playing   ride   run   sailing

Olivia: Do you like ¹ _____ football, Liam?

Liam: It's OK – I don't ² _____ it, but I can't ³ _____ very fast.

Olivia: What's your favourite sport?

Liam: I love sailing – but I ⁴ _____ like swimming! What about you?

Olivia: I like horse riding. ⁵ _____ you ⁶ _____ a horse?

Liam: No, I ⁷ _____ . Can you teach me?

Olivia: Sure!

VOCABULARY

1 Complete the sentences with the words in the box.

hit   jump   kick   ride   sail   score

1 When we go cycling in the mountains, I _____ my dad's bike.

2 My cousins can play football really well. They _____ a lot of goals.

3 In tennis, you need to _____ the ball really hard.

4 I want to _____ in a boat, but we don't live near the sea.

5 Our dog's good at football. He can _____ a ball.

6 Basketball players can _____ really high.

2 Read the description and complete the words.

1 This is a place where you swim.
swim_____   p_____

2 You can win this in a competition.
pr_____

3 It's a place where you can do different sports.
sp_____   ce_____

4 Sudoku is an example of this.
pu_____

5 You go fast with these on your feet.
ro_____   sk_____

6 Two people play this game on a board.
ch_____

SELF-ASSESSMENT!

How confident do you feel about:

- using *can* and *can't*? ☹ 😕 😐 ☺
- using *love, like, don't mind, don't like* and *hate*? ☹ 😕 😐 ☺
- talking about sports and games? ☹ 😕 😐 ☺

GIVING A PRESENTATION

1 TALKING SLOWLY AND CLEARLY

My partner is:

Other ideas/situations

Why are people sometimes hard to understand when they speak?

too fast   too quiet   head down

not opening mouth

Any other ideas? Think of real situations.

How do you feel when you can't understand a speaker?

Things I need to remember when I speak:
- Don't speak fast.
- _____
- _____
- _____

2 USING BODY LANGUAGE AND MAKING EYE CONTACT

How can body language help me communicate?
- hands? _____
- eyes? _____
- body? _____
- _____

3 PLANNING YOUR PRESENTATION

Today I want to talk about my favourite sport: _____.

⬇

Where and when I play:

⬇

Who plays with me:

⬇

How I/we play:

⬇

Why I like it:

⬇

Thanks for listening.

CHECKLIST

Speaking clearly	Me	My partner
Body language and eye contact		

UNIT 5 EVERY DAY'S A NEW DAY!

VOCABULARY
DAILY ROUTINES

1 Complete the phrases for daily routines with the verbs in the box.

> brush do go have meet play practise watch

 _____ a film

 _____ breakfast

 _____ to bed

 _____ my teeth

 _____ my homework

 _____ my friends

 _____ dance moves

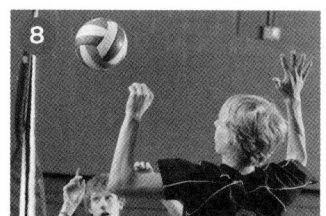 _____ sports

2 Choose the correct words to complete the sentences.

1 Before we make a video, we always practise our dance *moves / homework*.
2 After school, I meet my friends to play *lunch / sports*.
3 In the evening, I have *dinner / a film* with my family.
4 In the morning, I like having a cold *teeth / shower*. It wakes me up!
5 When I go *to bed / up* late, I feel tired in the morning.
6 I love going to the cinema to watch *breakfast / a film*.

3 Complete the text with the missing words.

HAVE YOU GOT A NORMAL SCHOOL DAY?   Home Forum 🔍

Not really! My parents work at a school, so we live there too. At the weekend, I ¹ g_____ u_____ early because on Saturday morning I ² p_____ sp_____ with my friends. In the evening, I go back to the school and I often ³ w_____ a f_____ with my family.

I think so! I live in Costa Rica and I ⁴ h_____ br_____ very early because school starts at 6.45 am. I ⁵ m_____ my fr_____ and we walk to school together. We ⁶ h_____ l_____ at school. It's always delicious and healthy.

I'm not sure! After school I look after my grandma, and she looks after me. We ⁷ h_____ d_____ together and then I ⁸ d_____ my h_____. She often helps me. I ⁹ g_____ to b_____ at about 10.30 pm.

WHAT'S THE TIME?

4 Match the clocks to the sentences.

a It's twelve o'clock. _____

b It's ten to one. _____

c It's quarter past two. _____

d It's quarter to eight. _____

e It's half past nine. _____

f It's twenty five past eleven. _____

5 Complete the sentences so they are true for you. Write the times in words.

On a school day I get up at ¹ _____.
I have lunch at ² _____ and I have dinner at ³ _____. I go to bed at ⁴ _____.
On holiday, I get up at ⁵ _____ and I have breakfast at ⁶ _____. I go to bed at ⁷ _____.

READING

SHORT TEXTS

1 What's an online school? Why do think some students go to school online?

_____

2 Read the texts in the exam task. Why do Adam and Magda go to online schools?

Adam: _____

Magda: _____

EXAM TIP

There is sometimes a word in the question which is also in one of the texts. However, this text is not always the correct answer.

3 Look at questions 1–4 in the exam task. <u>Underline</u> words in the texts that are in these questions.

☑ EXAM TRAINING READING PART 2

4 For each question, choose the correct answer.

		Adam	Magda
1	Who likes talking to people from other countries?	A	B
2	Who meets their friends at the weekend?	A	B
3	Who has a problem with their computer?	A	B
4	Who doesn't like doing homework?	A	B

WHAT'S FOR BREAKFAST?

ADAM

I hate talking to big groups, so I like being in an online school. There aren't many students in my online class and they are all from different parts of my country. I get up, have a shower and lessons start. After school, I do my homework. It isn't fun, but I know it's important. On Saturdays, I play sports outside with my friends.

MAGDA

I'm in an online school because I live on a farm. There aren't any schools near me. I love speaking to people from all over the world. We do our homework together – it's fun! The teachers are great, and the lessons are good, but my computer is slow. And I only meet my friends in the school holidays! 😕

5 **Critical Thinking** Write a list of three good and three bad things about studying at an online school. Use the texts and your own ideas.

GRAMMAR

PRESENT SIMPLE AND ADVERBS OF FREQUENCY

1 Choose the correct words to complete the sentences.

1 We *play / plays* chess after school.
2 I *meet / meets* my friends on Friday afternoons.
3 School *start / starts* at 8.30 am.
4 My friends *go / goes* to bed at 10 pm.
5 Our sports coach *run / runs* five km every morning.
6 My mum *have / has* lunch at work.
7 They *practise / practises* dance moves in the park.
8 Dario *brushes / brush* his teeth after breakfast.

2 Correct the sentences with the information in brackets.

1 I get up at 8 o'clock. (9 o'clock).
   I don't get up at 8 o'clock. I get up at 9 o'clock.

2 My sister likes swimming in the swimming pool. (in the sea)
   _____

3 We ride our bikes on Saturday morning. (Saturday afternoon)
   _____

4 My friends watch films at the cinema. (on TV)
   _____

5 My grandpa drinks milk for breakfast. (juice)
   _____

6 You play the piano well. (the guitar)
   _____

7 My dad goes to bed early. (late)
   _____

8 My lessons start at 7.30 in the morning. (8.30)
   _____

3 Complete the post with the present simple form of the verbs in brackets.

What's your school day like?

@Supergirl777

I'm Fay and I live in Nairobi, Kenya. I ¹ _____ (get up) early every morning. My brother ² _____ (go) to get some water and we ³ _____ (have) breakfast. I ⁴ _____ (not eat) very much, usually bread or fruit with a cup of hot tea. My brother and I ⁵ _____ (walk) to school, but it ⁶ _____ (not be) very near our home. My grandma ⁷ _____ (have) got a fruit and vegetable shop. When school ⁸ _____ (finish), I help her. When there aren't any people in the shop, I do my homework.

4 Write sentences with the adverbs and the phrases in the box.

> catch a ball   have breakfast   play board games
> play the piano   ride a horse   score a goal

1 often – she
  She often scores a goal.

2 always – we
  _____

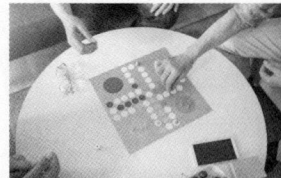

3 never – my friends
  _____

4 usually – our dog
  _____

5 sometimes – I
  _____

6 often – he
  _____

PRESENT SIMPLE QUESTIONS

5 Put the words in the correct order to make questions. Then write the short answers.

1 walk / to school / you / Do / ?
   Do you walk to school?
   (✓) _____ *Yes, I do.* _____

2 you and your family / Do / have dinner / usually / at 7 pm / ?
   _____
   (✓) _____

3 comic books / read / your best friend / Does / ?
   _____
   (✗) _____

4 play / your friends / Do / rugby / ?
   _____
   (✓) _____

5 start / Does / at 9 o'clock / your school / ?
   _____
   (✓) _____

6 at the cinema / you and your friends / Do / often / meet / ?
   _____
   (✗) _____

6 Complete the conversation with the present simple form of the verbs in brackets.

Hanna: [1] _____ you _____ (get up) at 7 o'clock at the weekend?

Amir: Yes, I [2] _____. I often ride my bike with my cousin on Saturday morning.

Hanna: Where [3] _____ you _____ (go)?

Amir: We sometimes ride to the beach. My cousin [4] _____ (love) swimming in the sea, but I [5] _____ (not like) it.

Hanna: [6] _____ your family _____ (stay) at home in the afternoon?

Amir: No, we [7] _____. We [8] _____ (usually / meet) my grandparents at a café.

7 ⟫ STRETCH! Write your answers to the questions in Exercise 5.

1 *No, I don't. I go to school by bus.*
2 _____
3 _____
4 _____
5 _____
6 _____

VOCABULARY

TRANSPORT AND TRAVEL

1 Find nine transport words in the word snake.

bustrainlorryhelicoptermotorbikeplanetractorboatcar

2 Complete the lists with eight words from Exercise 1. What's the missing word?

Road

Sky

Sea

3 Choose the correct words to complete the sentences.

1 Sailing in a *boat / bus* is fun when the weather is good.
2 I'm at the station. I've got a ticket for the 10 o'clock *train / lorry*.
3 Our cousins can drive a *tractor / helicopter* because they live on a farm.
4 The *bus / plane* takes about two hours to travel from Paris to Rome.
5 That's my *teacher's car / motorbike*. He rides it to school.

WRITING

A SOCIAL MEDIA POST

1 Think about your perfect day. Write your activities in part 1 of the table.

	Me	Noemi
In the morning	*get up at …*	
In the afternoon		
In the evening		

2 Read Noemi's social media post. Complete her part of the table in Exercise 1.

Noe@Noemi147

Hey everyone!

On a perfect day, I don't usually get up until 9 o'clock and then I have a big breakfast. I often meet my friends in the park. We sometimes ride our bikes, but we never play football – I can't kick a ball! In the afternoon, my dad makes pizza for us. And in the evening, I watch a film or play board games with my family.

Tell me about your perfect day!

3 Write a reply to Noemi's post. Use your notes in Exercise 1 and Noemi's post to help you.

LISTENING

A MONOLOGUE

1 You will hear a boy talking about his school in India. Read the notes in the exam task. What kind of word is missing in each gap? Is it a word, a number, a date or a time?

0 ___*number*___   2 _____

1 _____   3 _____

☑ **EXAM TRAINING**   LISTENING PART 2

2 🔊 5.01 **For each question, write the correct answer in the gap. Write one word or a number or a date or a time.**

You will hear a boy talking about his school in India.

> **Aditya's school**
>
> Students start school when they're:
> (0) _____6_____
>
> School year begins in:
> (1) _____
>
> Aditya and his sister get up at:
> (2) _____ am
>
> Aditya's favourite thing at school:
> (3) _____

3 🎓 Creative Thinking **Complete the notes for your own perfect school.**

My perfect school
Students start school when they're:

School year begins in:

It finishes in:

I get up at:

I travel to school by:

Favourite thing at school:

UNIT 5 REVIEW

GRAMMAR

1 Complete the text with the present simple form of the verbs in brackets.

On Saturday morning, I ¹_____ (get up) early but in our home we ²_____ (not have) breakfast. My sister always ³_____ (have) a shower and I ⁴_____ (practise) the guitar. Then we ⁵_____ (go) to my uncle's café. He ⁶_____ (not make) breakfast for us – he makes brunch. That's breakfast and lunch together!

2 Put the words in the correct order.

1 by train / My parents / travel / always / .
_____

2 hiking / with my family / never / I / go / .
_____

3 doesn't / My dad / at home / have lunch / usually / .
_____

4 watch films / don't / I / at the cinema / often / .
_____

5 go / sometimes / late / We / to bed / .
_____

6 often / with me / football / Our dog / plays / .
_____

3 Complete the questions with the verbs in the box. Then complete the short answers.

brush   do   go   meet   play   watch

1 _____ your mum _____ to bed late?
No, _____.

2 _____ you _____ the guitar in a band?
No, _____.

3 _____ you and your friends sometimes _____ a film in class?
Yes, _____.

4 _____ your brother _____ his friends after school?
No, _____.

5 _____ your friends always _____ their homework?
Yes, _____.

6 _____ you _____ your teeth after breakfast?
Yes, _____.

VOCABULARY

1 Choose the correct words to complete the text.

On a school day, I ¹*get / go* up at 7 o'clock and I have breakfast. Then I ²*get / have* a shower and I ³*do / brush* my teeth. After school I often ⁴*meet / play* sports. Sometimes I ⁵*practise / play* dance moves. At 10 o'clock, I ⁶*get / go* to bed.

2 Complete the transport and travel words.

1 My aunt drives all day for work. She drives a big l_ _ _ _.
2 We want to sail in a b_ _ _ across the Mediterranean Sea.
3 Can you hear the h_ _ _ _ _ _ _ _ up in the sky?
4 When I'm older, I want to ride a fast m_ _ _ _ _ _ _ _.
5 We've got a t_ _ _ _ _ _ to help with the work on our farm.
6 I love travelling by t_ _ _ _. It's fast and I can look out of the window.

SELF-ASSESSMENT!

How confident do you feel about:
• using adverbs of frequency?   ☹ ☺ ☺ ☺
• using the present simple?   ☹ ☺ ☺ ☺
• talking about your daily routine?   ☹ ☺ ☺ ☺
• telling the time?   ☹ ☺ ☺ ☺
• talking about transport and travel?   ☹ ☺ ☺ ☺

IT'S GOOD TO DO NEW THINGS!

1 THINK

My group is:

Work together on one word map and think of lots of ideas.

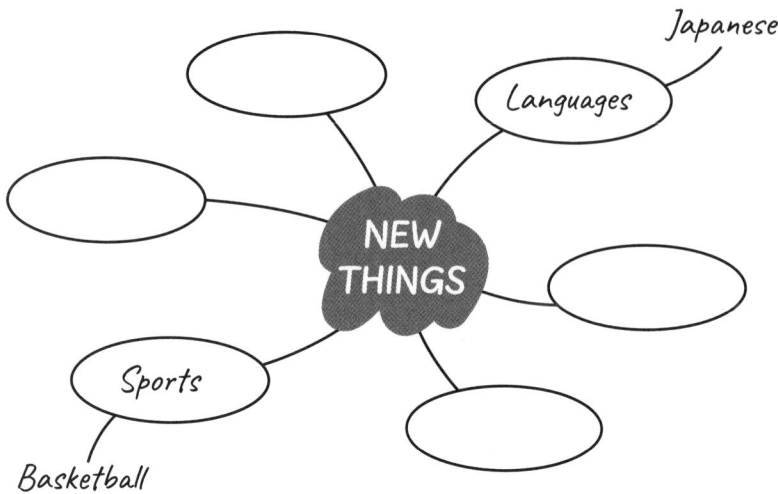

Japanese

Languages

NEW THINGS

Sports

Basketball

Remember, these are things that are <u>new</u> for every person in your group.

Tip for Think

Make sure to include ideas from everyone in the group. It doesn't matter if you don't all agree.

2 PREPARE

Things we can do every day:

_____ _____

Choose some activities from your spidergram.

Our activity for the presentation is:

_____

Choose one that you all agree on.

Why do we want to do this new activity? _____

_____

Things we need to do the activity: _____

_____

Where we can do it: _____

When we can do it: _____

Other information: _____

_____

Tips for Prepare

Think about things you need to find out. Where can you get this information? Decide who will look for it.

3 DEVELOP

Our roles:

Giving the presentation: (Who? One person or two?)

_____

Making the video: (Who? One person or two?)

_____

What we need for the presentation:

_____

_____

Get these things ready!

Tips for Develop

If you have two presenters, decide who says what. If you have two people making the video, decide how one person can help the other.

4 PRESENT

Practise your video presentation first and look at it together.

Good things:	Things we can improve:

Questions for other groups:

_____

_____

_____

You can make short notes when you listen to other groups' presentations.

Tips for Present

Presenter(s): remember to speak slowly and clearly. Look at the camera, not the floor!

SELF-EVALUATION

I can ...
- think of new activities I can do ◯
- share information about one activity and do research to find out more about it. ◯
- work with my group to plan a video presentation and agree on our roles. ◯
- make the video presentation and show it to the classs. ◯

PRONUNCIATION

UNIT 1

STRESS IN SENTENCES WITH THE VERB *BE*

1 🔊 **1.2 Listen and repeat.**

1 He's **twelve**.
2 **Parties** are **fun**.
3 We **aren't** at **school** today.
4 She **isn't** in my **class**.
5 Is your **favourite colour blue**?
6 Are you from **Egypt**?

2 🔊 **1.3 <u>Underline</u> the stressed words in the sentences.**

1 They're beautiful.
2 Are you in this class?
3 I'm not from Spain.
4 Is she the teacher?
5 We're thirteen.
6 It isn't cheap.
7 He's my friend.
8 We aren't at school.

3 🔊 **1.3 Listen, check and repeat.**

UNIT 2

PAIRS OF WORDS WITH *AND*

1 🔊 **2.2 Listen and repeat.**

> mother and father   uncle and aunt
> family and friends

2 **Read the sentences and <u>underline</u> which words link together.**

1 Your brothers and sisters are happy.
2 He's tall and dark.
3 My brothers are Josh and Danny.
4 My grandpa and grandma have got a cat.
5 Her son and daughter are twins.
6 My uncle and cousins are here.

3 🔊 **2.3 Listen, check and repeat.**

UNIT 3

WORD STRESS / SYLLABLES IN WORDS

1 🔊 **3.2 Listen and repeat.**

juice   chocolate   strawberries

2 **How many syllables do the words have? Draw a circle for each syllable, like the ones in Exercise 1.**

1 salad	2 oranges	3 bowl
4 noodles	5 plate	6 vegetables
7 milkshake	8 bottle	9 sugar

3 🔊 **3.2 Listen, check and repeat.**

UNIT 4

CAN / CAN'T

1 🔊 **4.2 Listen and repeat.**

She can **sail**.   I **can't swim**.

2 🔊 **4.3 Listen and circle the word you hear.**

1 We *can / can't* play football.
2 Kris *can / can't* run fast.
3 My parents *can / can't* speak English very well.
4 We *can / can't* ride our bikes to school.
5 Alex *can / can't* jump very high.
6 My dog *can / can't* catch a ball.

3 🔊 **4.3 Listen again and repeat.**

UNIT 5

/s/, /z/ AND /ɪz/ WITH PRESENT SIMPLE ENDINGS

1 🔊 **5.2 Listen to the endings of the words and repeat.**

/s/	/z/	/ɪz/
get**s**	doe**s**	practic**es**
meet**s**	ha**s**	watch**es**

2 **Put the verbs in the correct place in the table.**

> brushes catches plays goes stops
> takes travels walks washes

/s/	/z/	/ɪz/

3 🔊 **5.3 Listen, check and repeat.**

This page is intentionally blank.

VOCABULARY BUILDER

UNIT 1 MY VOCABULARY

FAVOURITE THINGS; DESCRIBING THINGS

1 Find the words in the wordsearch.

B	B	A	N	D	A	C	C	H	B
I	F	G	U	I	T	A	R	S	O
G	R	Q	U	F	E	L	I	P	A
A	X	U	C	A	M	E	R	A	R
I	B	M	I	S	K	L	A	R	D
D	I	C	N	T	R	N	U	T	G
D	K	Y	E	G	W	E	B	Y	A
Z	E	H	M	P	V	W	D	T	M
O	G	Z	A	N	J	L	U	F	E
C	O	M	I	C	B	O	O	K	N
P	K	S	A	S	L	O	W	E	M

2 Look at the photos and write the words from the wordsearch.

 s_____

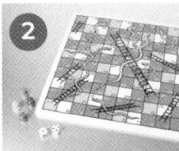 b_____

 g_____

 f_____

 c_____

 c_____

 p_____

 b_____

 n_____

 b_____

 b_____

 c_____

UNIT 2 MY VOCABULARY

FAMILY MEMBERS; DESCRIBING PEOPLE

 mum

 aunt

 grandpa

 cousin

 sister

 uncle

 brother

 dad

1 Match the photos (a–h) to the descriptions (1–8).

1 He's young but he's tall. He's got short, curly hair. It's dark.

2 He's 42 years old. He's short and he's got long, straight hair.

3 He's tall. He's got short, curly hair. It's dark. He's 38.

4 Her hair is long and straight. She's tall and she's 36 years old.

5 His hair is short and curly. He's 70, so he's quite old.

6 She's got dark hair. It's short and straight. She's at university.

7 Her hair is short and curly. She's 14 years old and she's short.

8 She's 45. She's got blonde hair. It's long and curly.

FOOD, DRINK AND CONTAINERS; NUMBERS 20–100

1 Use the number code in the table to find the answers.

twenty-one	thirty	thirty-eight	forty-one	forty-seven	fifty-nine
sixty-five	seventy-seven	seventy-nine	eighty-eight	ninety-five	a hundred

1 bowl + plate = _____21 + 38_____ = _____59_____ = _____juice_____
2 noodles + sandwich = _____ = _____ = _____
3 bottle – bowl = _____ = _____ = _____
4 noodles + vegetables = _____ = _____ = _____
5 vegetables + milkshake = _____ = _____ = _____
6 juice – plate = _____ = _____ = _____
7 fruit – noodles = _____ = _____ = _____
8 glass – milkshake = _____ = _____ = _____

UNIT 4 MY VOCABULARY

SPORTS AND GAMES VERBS; SPORTS AND GAMES NOUNS

1 Write the sports words. Then match them with the photos.

1 EBONUC   `B O U N C E`
2 RNU
3 WHTRO
4 CTCAH
5 SMWI
6 SOERC
7 CKIK
8 DREI
9 AWKL
10 UJMP
11 HTI
12 LSIA

2 One word is wrong in each sentence. Find and correct the mistake.

1 Our team is in a football puzzle with other schools. _____
2 People swim and play basketball and tennis at the sports pool. _____
3 There are always two prizes in a game of chess. _____
4 I go fast when I wear my swimming skates. _____

DAILY ROUTINES; WHAT'S THE TIME?; TRANSPORT AND TRAVEL

1 Write six funny sentences. Use one word from each shape.

brush
do
go
have
meet
play
practise
watch

a film
a shower
breakfast
dance moves
dinner
lunch
my friends
my homework
my teeth
sports
to bed

on a …
boat
bus
helicopter
motorbike
plane
tractor
train

at …
half past
o'clock
quarter past
quarter to

one
two
three
four
five
six
seven
eight
nine
ten
eleven
twelve

I brush my teeth on a helicopter at eight o'clock.

1 _____
2 _____
3 _____
4 _____
5 _____
6 _____

2 Now choose one of your sentences and draw a picture.

08:00 AM

MY STUDY JOURNAL

UNITS 1 AND 2

1 Find 12 vocabulary items from Unit 1 in the word spiral.

Which is your favourite?

boardgamefilmcyclingonlinegamingguitareeighteenelevenhikingninepartybikeband

This isn't a test! Look in your Student's Book if you can't remember.

2 Complete the sentences about the vocabulary in Exercise 1 with numbers.

There are _____ objects.
There are _____ activities.
There are _____ numbers.

3 One of the items in Exercise 1 begins with C. Write more words you know that begin with C here.

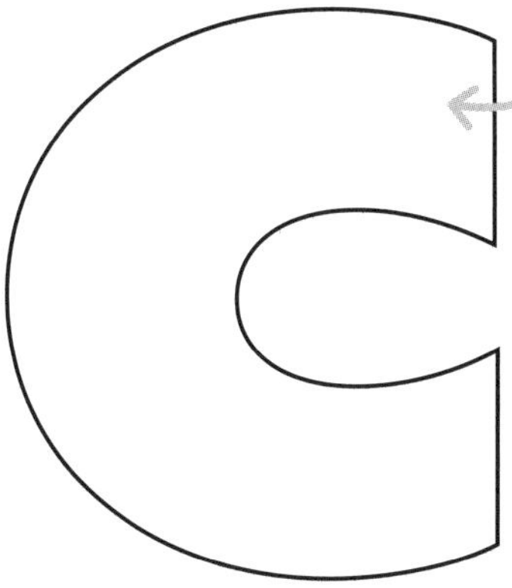

C

4 Draw these things:
- a young boy with short, curly hair
- a beautiful, big tree

5 Now use adjectives to describe these drawings.

1 _____

2 _____

3 _____

4 _____

6 What is the missing word in each puzzle?

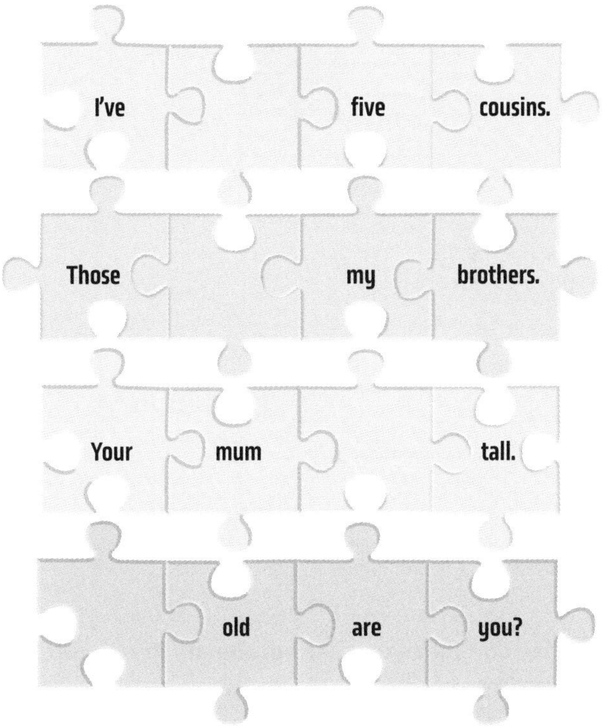

| I've | five | cousins. |

| Those | my | brothers. |

| Your | mum | tall. |

| old | are | you? |

Now use your imagination and write two more puzzles.

7 Are these sentences true or false? Correct the mistakes in the false sentences.

1 My sister's mother is my aunt.
2 My mother's father is my grandpa.
3 Your brother is your parents' daughter.
4 Their dad's parents are their aunt and uncle.
5 His cousins are his uncle's children.

UNITS 3 AND 4

1 Do the food quiz. You have three minutes. How many words can you think of?

A food you eat from a bowl
B food vegetarians eat
C drinks we put in a glass
D food with gluten
E fruit

2 Write verbs connected with the two pictures below.

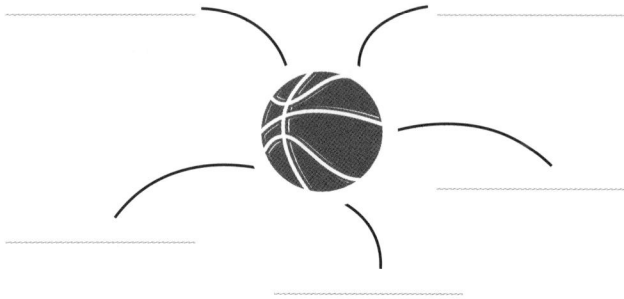

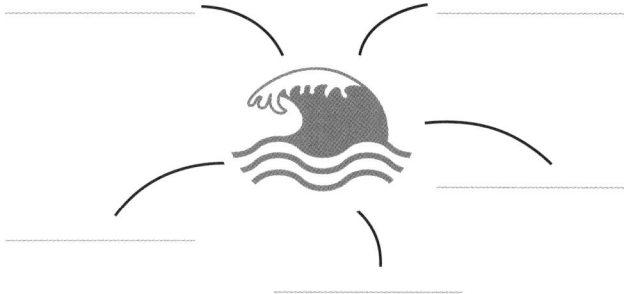

3 Play dominoes to make vocabulary items with two words.

skates | sports

free | swimming

centre | chess

board | gluten-

pool | roller

4 Complete the questions and answers about food with the words in the bowl. Then match the questions to the answers.

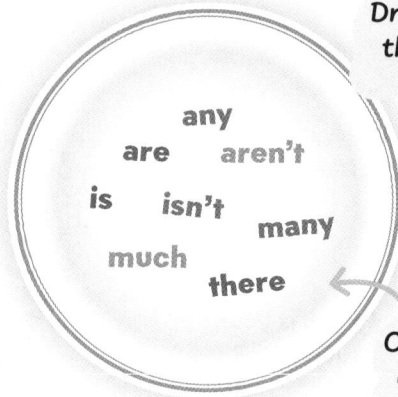

Draw lines between the questions and the answers!

any
are   aren't
is   isn't
many
much
there

Clue: there is one extra word you don't need.

QUESTIONS
1 How _____ cheese is there? ____
2 _____ there any noodles? ____
3 How _____ tomatoes are there? ____
4 _____ there any milk? ____

ANSWERS
a Yes, but there _____ many.
b There isn't _____ cheese!
c Yes, but there _____ much.
d _____ are a lot.

Which questions have countable nouns?

_____

Which questions have uncountable nouns?

_____

5 Separate the words to make sentences. Then change them so they are true for you.

1 Myfrienddoesn'tlikeplayingvideogames.

_____

2 Thereisn'tanychocolateinourhouse.

_____

3 Lucacan'tjumpwithaskateboard.

_____

4 Therearesixteensportsteamsinmyschool.

_____

5 Leodoesn'tlikeplayinggolfbuthelikeswatchingit.

_____

6 Mayacan'teatwheatpastabutshecaneatrice.

_____

6 Which sentences (1–6) are about ....

1 ability: _____ _____
2 quantity: _____ _____
3 likes and dislikes: _____ _____

1 **Write your daily routine activities connected to the rooms.**

Bathroom	Living room	Bedroom	Kitchen
go to bed			

2 **Draw the times on the clocks. What times are they on a digital watch?**

1   half past three

2   quarter to eight

3   five o'clock

3 **Draw three more clocks and put the times on them. Write what time it is.**

4 **Put the words in the correct order. Then answer the questions.**

1   you / usually / How / to / do / school / go / ?

_____

2   time / lunch / you / What / have / do / ?

_____

3   lot / Do / you / a / clothes / buy / of / ?

_____

4   do / homework / do / Where / your / you / ?

_____

5   an / town / Does / have / your/ airport / ?

_____

6   What / weekend / usually / do / at / you / do / the / ?

_____

Acknowledgements

The authors and publishers acknowledge the following sources of copyright material and are grateful for the permissions granted. While every effort has been made, it has not always been possible to identify the sources of all the material used, or to trace all copyright holders. If any omissions are brought to our notice, we will be happy to include the appropriate acknowledgements on reprinting and in the next update to the digital edition, as applicable.

Key: U = Unit, VB = Vocabulary Builder, SJ: Study Journal.

Student Book

The publishers are grateful to the following contributors: EMC, text design and layouts; Daniel Summersgill, cover design; Sonica Studios, audio recordings; Silversun Media Group, video production; STEAM sections, Joanna Haywood; Oracy consultant, Michelle Mahony; Editorial work, Melissa Wilson, Joanne Kent, Jenny Smith and Alicia McAuley; Exam reviewer, Yvonne Dagan.

Photography

All the photos are sourced from Getty Images.

U1: kali9/E+; Science Photo Library; Ryan McVay/Photodisc; Kitthita Methakornthitiporn/iStock/Getty Images Plus; Erik_V/iStock/Getty Images Plus; Designer_things/iStock/Getty Images Plus; monkeybusinessimages/iStock/Getty Images Plus; LSOphoto/iStock/Getty Images Plus; wundervisuals/E+; shironosov/iStock/Getty Images Plus; Addictive Stock/iStock/Getty Images Plus; Proximo/iStock/Getty Images Plus; eclipse_images/E+; Imgorthand/E+; Akimasa Harada/Moment; ArtistGNDphotography/E+; Iuliia Anisimova/iStock/Getty Images Plus; Westend61; CraigRJD/iStock/Getty Images Plus; normallens/iStock/Getty Images Plus; Serg Semin/500px; Thomas Winz/The Image Bank; real444/E+; Photobalance/iStock/Getty Images Plus; Lorado/E+; IP Galanternik D.U./E+; golero/E+; FatCamera/iStock/Getty Images Plus; skaman306/Moment; brusinski/E+; Inti St Clair/DigitalVision; **U2:** FatCamera/E+; Variety; Richard Drury/DigitalVision; PamelaJoeMcFarlane/E+; Klaus Vedfelt/DigitalVision; Larysa Vdovychenko/Moment; MoMo Productions/Stone; Morsa Images/DigitalVision; Jose Luis Pelaez Inc/DigitalVision; pkline/E+; Westend61; JohnnyGreig/E+; NadyaPhoto/iStock/Getty Images Plus; MILATAS; LaylaBird/E+; Frazao Studio Latino/E+; Igor Alecsander/E+; **U3:** miodrag ignjatovic/E+; Morsa Images/DigitalVision; visualspace/E+; Kong Ding Chek/E+; ibeyphoto/iStock/Getty Images Plus; OlgaKorica/iStock/Getty Images Plus; Image Professionals GmbH/Foodcollection; Arundhati Sathe/iStock/Getty Images Plus; rezza anggita putra/iStock/Getty Images Plus; Tetra Images/Tetra images; Dove Lee/Moment; Dmytro Gilitukha/500px Plus; Claire Plumridge/Moment; Judith Haeusler/Image Source; Razvan Dinu/500px; Chris Clor/Tetra images; Rebeca Mello/Moment; FotografiaBasica/E+; Deborah Pendell/Moment Open; FanPro/Moment; Jacky Parker Photography/Moment; Nicholas Kostin/Moment; Drazen_/E+; luchezar/E+; Westend61; **U4:** Tom Wilde/Stone; Olha Romaniuk/iStock/Getty Images Plus; Anna Savina/iStock/Getty Images Plus; Cavan Images; akrp/iStock/Getty Images Plus; Fran Polito/Moment; artpartner-images/The Image Bank; Aflo Images; shih-wei/E+; Westend61; Peter Cade/Photodisc; kali9/iStock/Getty Images Plus; FamVeld/iStock/Getty Images Plus; Mike Harrington/Stone; Ben Welsh/The Image Bank; jxfzsy/E+; Cavan Images; Alicia Llop/Moment; Steve Baccon/The Image Bank; Baac3nes/Moment; Kmatta/Moment; SolStock/E+; Mario Marco/Moment; miljko/E+; motimeiri/iStock/Getty Images Plus; Witthaya Prasongsin/Moment; Richard Drury/DigitalVision; Daniel Milchev/The Image Bank; Tara Moore/Stone; Stefan Cristian Cioata/Moment; Jacob Wackerhausen/iStock/Getty Images Plus; IPGGutenbergUKLtd/iStock/Getty Images Plus; **U5:** Riska/E+; Ekaterina Podrezova/Moment; Darren Robb/The Image Bank; nortonrsx/iStock/Getty Images Plus; monkeybusinessimages/iStock/Getty Images Plus; SDI Productions/E+; shironosov/iStock/Getty Images Plus; Dougal Waters/DigitalVision; SolStock/E+; YinYang/iStock/Getty Images Plus; Elva Etienne/Moment; fcafotodigital/E+; bernie_photo/E+; Christopher Ames/E+; MoMo Productions/DigitalVision; Â©Studio One-One/Moment; Ippei Naoi/Moment; Kryssia Campos/Moment; Patryce Bak/Stone; MarioGuti/iStock/Getty Images Plus; Uditha Weliwita/500px; Allan Baxter/The Image Bank; Nisangha/iStock/Getty Images Plus; Eplisterra/iStock/Getty Images Plus; Westend61; dreamnikon/iStock/Getty Images Plus; oticki/iStock/Getty Images Plus; Johner Images/Johner Images Royalty-Free; Dmitro2009/iStock/Getty Images Plus; Martin Ruegner/Stone; Jackyenjoyphotography/Moment; Tetra Images/Tetra images; Southern Lightscapes-Australia/Moment; MEDITERRANEAN/E+; **Steam Investigations:** FatCamera/E+; ttsz/iStock/Getty Images Plus; Westend61; gyener/DigitalVision Vectors; diane555/DigitalVision Vectors; Ada daSilva/DigitalVision Vectors; Peter Cade/Stone; _lolik_/iStock/Getty Images Plus; Tim Robberts/Stone; Julia Lemba/iStock/Getty Images Plus; Photos by R A Kearton/Moment; Mark Chivers/Moment; Sarah Walton/500px; Fiona McAllister Photography/Moment; Alexandra Jursova/Moment; charliebishop/E+; **Grammar Reference And Practice:** Yevhen Borysov/Moment; kolotuschenko/iStock/Getty Images Plus; Merve Ozkaya/DigitalVision Vectors; filo/DigitalVision Vectors.

Cover photography by Rockaa/E+/Getty Images; Karl Hendon/Moment/Getty Images.

Videos

Video production by Silversun Media Group.

Video stills (grammar animations, grammar vlogs, oracy videos & speaking videos) by Silversun Media Group.

Audio

Audio produced by Sonica Studios.

Illustrations

U2, U3: Virginia Fontanabona; Gergely Forizs; **U4:** Virginia Fontanabona; **U5:** Virginia Fontanabona; Dani Geremia; **Grammar Reference and Practice:** Javier Joaquin (The Organisation); Humberto Blanco (Sylvie Poggio Artists Agency); Gary Parsons; Adz (Sylvie Poggio Artists Agency); **Steam Investigations:** Martin Sanders; Virginia Fontanabona; Gergely Forizs.

Typeset

Typesetting by eMC Design.

Workbook

The publishers are grateful to the following contributors: EMC, text design and layouts; Daniel Summersgill, cover design; Sonica Studios, audio recordings; Vicki Anderson, Pronunciation and Study Journal; Jessica Soltys, Meredith Levy and Ruth Cox, Editorial work; Yvonne Dagan, Exam reviewer.

Text

U1: Text about The Kanneh-Masons family. Copyright © The Kanneh-Masons. Reproduced with kind permission.

Photography

All the photographs are sourced from Getty Images.

U1: anocha98/iStock; Erik_V/iStock; alekseystemmer/iStock; Hugnoi/iStock; magda_istock/iStock; Peter Dazeley/The Image Bank; Piotrurakau/iStock; skynesher/E+; GibsonPictures/E+; Peathegee Inc/Tetra images; Richard Heathcote; nuiiko/iStock; Jupiterimages/Stockbyte; Imgorthand/E+; Johner Images/Johner Images; imaginima/E+; Sean Murphy/Stone; Photographer, Basak Gurbuz Derman/Moment; Anastasiia Yanishevska/iStock; Алексей Облов/Moment; Sergydv/iStock; Imgorthand/E+; Jupiterimages/Pixland; Iuliia Zavalishina/iStock; Flashvector/iStock; Fran Polito/Moment; Aleksei Morozov/iStock/Getty Images Plus; markOfshell/iStock/Getty Images Plus; Veysel Celikdemir/iStock/Getty Images Plus; **U2:** Westend61; AzmanL/E+; AnnaStills/iStock; Morsa Images/DigitalVision; MesquitaFMS/E+; Mehmet Hilmi Barcin/E+; Photodisc; Hiroyuki Ito/Hulton Archive; serebryannikov/iStock; Maskot; Oliver Rossi/DigitalVision; errlre/iStock; Stígur Már Karlsson/Heimsmyndir/E+; FatCamera/E+; Prostock-Studio/iStock; Yulia Sutyagina/iStock; **U3:** Evbokia Spure/iStock; Thorpe, Lara Jane/Foodcollection; Mariha-kitchen/iStock; umbertoleporini/iStock; Tatyana Kildisheva/Moment; Epkin/iStock; aluxum/E+; Clara Lambert/500px; kbeis/DigitalVision Vectors; Vectorig/DigitalVision Vectors; Georgiy Datsenko/iStock; ChamilleWhite/iStock; Dougal Waters/DigitalVision; helovi/iStock; xavierarnau/E+; Satoshi-K/E+; Senez/Moment; georgeclerk/E+; claire davidson/foap; Paweena Sae-ung/Moment; kevinjeon00/E+; Utamaru Kido/Moment; joSon/stone; South_agency/E+; Siempreverde22/iStock; Andrea Kennard Photography/Moment; appleuzr/DigitalVision Vectors; Thinkstock/Stockbyte; y-studio/iStock; OksanaKiian/iStock; Peter Dazeley/The Image Bank; Sadik Demiroz/Photodisc; Betka82/iStock; Naomi Rahim/Moment; Georgiy Datsenko/iStock/Getty Images Plus; Betka82/iStock/Getty Images Plus;**U4:** sonofpioneer/iStock; Sean Justice/The Image Bank; seksan Mongkhonkhamsao/Moment; PonyWang/E+; AscentXmedia/E+; goc/E+; moodboard/Connect Images; Mikael Vaisanen/The Image Bank; Mlenny/E+; Prykhodov/iStock; SteveLuker/iStock; taonga/iStock; Peter Dazeley/Getty Images News; Mariia Vitkovska/iStock; Leon Harris/Connect Images; MesquitaFMS/E+; Catherine Delahaye/Stone; skynesher/E+; Kristian Bell/Moment; ptaxa/E+; stephevans/iStock; LWA/Dann Tardif/DigitalVision; courtneyk/E+; Cyndi Monaghan/Moment; iluziaa/iStock; Olga Dobrovolska/Moment; Johner Images/Johner Images; **U5:** wundervisuals/E+; Vuk Saric/E+; FG Trade/E+; Imgorthand/E+; andresr/E+; kali9/E+; JackF/iStock; FatCamera/E+; Phynart Studio/E+; Halfpoint Images/Moment; vgajic/E+; Stefania Pelfini, La Waziya Photography/Moment; filmstudio/E+; Hannah_Walder/iStock; Zave Smith/Connect Images; hoozone/E+; Nick David/Photodisc; StockPlanets/E+; **VB:** Teddi Yaeger Photography/Moment; Creative Crop/Photodisc; 9parusnikov/iStock; Winfried Wisniewski/Photodisc; Frank Rothe/The Image Bank; VasiliyKozlov/iStock; Westend61; Thomas Barwick/DigitalVision; Aleksandr Zubkov/Moment; Kenny Williamson/Moment; Klaus Vedfelt/DigitalVision; Sean Gladwell/Moment; Sutthiwat Srikhrueadam/Moment; Whitestorm/iStock; takepicsforfun/iStock; Szakaly/iStock; Judy Unger/DigitalVision Vectors; Amguy/iStock; Jojo Wardjojo/500px; Buena Vista Images/DigitalVision; Creative Crop/DigitalVision; Aiselin82/iStock; Sam Armstrong/The Image Bank; Barks_japan/iStock; Nataliy Kl/iStock; Turac Novruzova/iStock; wongmbatuloyo/iStock; Graphic Stock/iStock; Mironov Konstantin/iStock; Ashva73/iStock; msan10/iStock; CSA Images; illust-monster/iStock; Gulay Erun/iStock; Fidan Babayeva/iStock; Massimo Borchi/Atlantide Phototravel/Corbis Documentary; Jedraszak/iStock; Arturo Rosenow/iStock; Alexander Fattal/iStock; owngarden/Moment; Mordolff/E+; Roc Canals/Moment; Marco_Piunti/E+; Gary Yeowell/DigitalVision; Mike Riley/Moment; EThamPhoto/The Image Bank; Laura Hedien/Moment; slowmotiongli/iStock; Jayanta Bordoloi/500px; Gary Chalker/Moment; dikkyoesin1/RooM; Anita Kot/Moment; dreamnikon/iStock; Olga Naumova/iStock; **SJ:** Flashpop/DigitalVision; Nevena Uzurov/Moment; mevans/E+; Andrey Danilovich/iStock; ithinksky/DigitalVision Vectors; mystockicons/DigitalVision Vectors; calvindexter/DigitalVision Vectors; kbeis/DigitalVision Vectors; drmakkoy/DigitalVision Vectors; cteconsulting/iStock.

Illustrations

U2: Javier Joaquin (Beehive Illustration); **U3**: Design; **VB:** Javier Joaquin (Beehive Illustration); Virginia Fontanabona (Beehive Illustration).

Audio

Audio produced by Sonica Studios.

Typeset

Typesetting by eMC Design.

URLs

The publisher has used its best endeavors to ensure that the URLs for external websites referred to in this book are correct and active at the time of going to press. However, the publisher has no responsibility for the websites and can make no guarantee that a site will remain live or that the content is or will remain appropriate.